DISCOVERING GOD'S STORY

FULLY ILLUSTRATED BIBLE HANDBOOK
IN CHRONOLOGICAL ORDER

Standard®
PUBLISHING

Cincinnati, Ohio

Published by Standard Publishing, Cincinnati, Ohio
www.standardpub.com

Printed in: China

Writer: Jim Eichenberger
Project editor: Lynn Lusby Pratt
Content editor: Cheryl Frey
Copy editor: Faith Watson
Consultants: Thanks to Dr. Robert Lowery, Professor of New Testament and Dean of Bible and Theology at Lincoln Christian University; Dr. V. Gilbert Beers, author of over 150 Bible-related books, former editor of *Christianity Today*; and other professors, editors, and ministry practitioners who provided valuable insight in shaping this volume.
Cover and interior design: Scott Ryan
Production: Robert E. Korth

Cover photos courtesy of www.dreamstime.com.
Photos on the following pages courtesy of www.istockphoto.com: 11—UFO, 12—Satan mask, 14, 23—map, 25—map, 35, 37—African people, 43, 59—war chariot, 67—Dagon, 90, 142.
Photos on the following pages courtesy of www.thinkstockphotos.com: 22, 23—rainbow, 25—African carving, 26, 27—yin yang, 30, 34, 62, 96, 106, 112, 144, 166—Spartacus, 189.
Photos on the following pages courtesy of www.flickr.com: 32, 115—Appian Way, 125, 128—riverbank, 151—Pools of Bethesda, 160, 170, 176.
Maps on the following pages are from *Standard Bible Atlas*, copyright © 2006, 2008 by Standard Publishing. All rights reserved. Pages: 37, 53, 61, 100, 145, 167, 207.
All other photos courtesy of en.wikipedia.org.

The Good Sam Club logo is a registered trademark of Affinity Group, Inc., Ventura, California, which is not affiliated with Standard Publishing.

ISBN 978-0-7847-2398-2

15 14 13 12 11 10   1 2 3 4 5 6 7 8 9

CONTENTS

OLD TESTAMENT

Chapter 1: Prehistory—*A perfect world is created, but it is marred with the intrusion of evil. God confronts evil, and people struggle with the issue of God's power, nature, and justice.*

Chapter 2: Patriarchs—*God begins to restore the entire world by creating a special nation that would bless all other nations.*

Chapter 3: Law and Land—*God gives his nation a homeland and creates a government in which he alone is king.*

Chapter 4: The United Kingdom—*God grants his people's demand for a human king, but they would find that mere mortals are not up to the task.*

Chapter 5: A Kingdom Divided—*Arrogance and rebellion result in a civil war that creates two very imperfect kingdoms.*

Chapter 6: Exile and Return—*Both kingdoms are judged, and God's people are forcibly removed from the land of promise. That is not the end of the story, only a necessary prelude to the concluding chapters.*

NEW TESTAMENT

Chapter 7: Jesus, the Promised King—*Four centuries of God's silence are broken when Jesus enters a broken world.*

Chapter 8: Jesus, the Comforter of the Afflicted—*In his ministry on earth, Jesus reaches out to even the lowest sectors of society, offering hope and wholeness.*

Chapter 9: Jesus, the Afflicter of the Comfortable—*In his ministry on earth, Jesus challenges established, self-serving religious authority.*

Chapter 10: Jesus, the Suffering Servant—*Jesus pays the price for the sins of the world and makes reconciliation with God possible.*

Chapter 11: Peter and the Early Church—*After Jesus ascends to Heaven, the early church grows and the apostle Peter becomes one of the church's powerful spokesmen.*

Chapter 12: Paul and the Early Church—*Paul, a zealous Jew who tries to destroy the church, becomes a Jesus follower and builds up the church around the known world.*

Chapter 13: Toward the End of the Story—*The work of the church continues toward completion. All who have accepted Jesus' invitation will enjoy eternal fellowship with God.*

APPENDICES

ABOUT *DISCOVERING GOD'S STORY*

Discovering God's Story is designed to help readers understand the Bible as one continuous story. It can be skimmed quickly to give a general overview. It can be pulled off the shelf countless times to aid anyone engaging in a deeper study of Scripture. It can be referenced during a sermon or Bible study for additional background information.

Each biblical event is explained by using the following features:

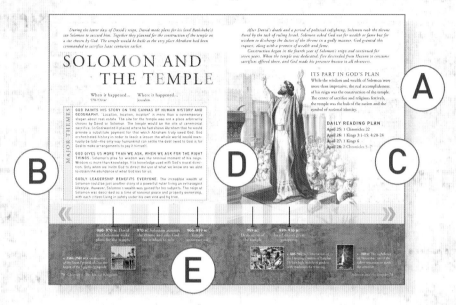

A = ITS PART IN GOD'S PLAN

Of course, not every biblical event is included in this book. But each event is described in a way that refers to events preceding it and foreshadows those events that follow.

B = MAJOR THEMES

The Bible was written at specific times in human history. It refers to specific events in the framework of human history. Yet the themes contained therein are timeless. For each event in this book, a few simple ageless applications are suggested.

C = DAILY READING PLAN

This section of the book is designed as a quick but thorough reference to the event described on each two-page spread. Certain Scriptures (and time line events) are shown in red to highlight what is central. The daily readings are formulated as a yearlong plan to also give readers a simple overview of God's entire story. Even though the plan runs from January through December, we recommend that a reader beginning the plan mid-year start from the beginning rather than the actual date. Many chronological plans that allow the user to read the *entire* Bible in a year are also available and are recommended after using the concise overview in this book.

D = STANDARD CLASSIC BIBLE ART

The illustrations in *Discovering God's Story* come from the Standard Classic Bible Art collection. In 1908 Standard Publishing went to the art schools of Europe to embark on an ambitious mission. They would commission the creation of oil paintings that depicted all the major events of the Bible. Over the next forty years, more than eight hundred works were completed by some of the more capable painters of that day.

These images have appeared in all sorts of publications over the decades and have become familiar to many people. They vary in style and (like almost all biblical art) sometimes more accurately depict the time in which they were painted than the event they represent, but they are some of the most cherished Christian art of the early twentieth century. Standard Publishing still possesses the original oils, and digitally restored images of the paintings are available only from www.standardpub.com/bibleart/.

E = TIME LINE

When studying the Bible, it is important to recognize that Scripture itself affirms that it is not a collection of myths or a series of visions. Rather, the Bible says it is an account of real events happening at real places at specific times.

For that reason, the time line includes dated events occurring outside the Bible account but at the same time as biblical events. Some information in the time line is in the form of lists or facts that are related in some way to biblical events.

Ancient dates are not always easy to fix exactly, so many are approximations based on available information. There may be disagreement among historians on many dates. Dating Bible events has raised some unique controversies and questions. *Discovering God's Story* uses some specific dates but recognizes that arguments exist for alternatives.

- *Bishop Ussher and dating prehistory*—James Ussher, an archbishop in the Church of Ireland in the mid-seventeenth century, developed a time line for the earliest biblical events. Bishop Ussher argued that creation occurred in 4004 BC. He also attached dates to the great flood, the tower of Babel, and other events described in the first eleven chapters of Genesis. The issues involved in this dating system, and its implications for other controversies such as young-earth vs. old-earth creationism, are worthy of deeper discussion than allowed for in a volume such as this. Therefore, our time line simply denotes these events as happening before recorded history.

- *Dates of the patriarchs and Moses*—Traditional Bible chronology places Abram entering into Canaan at the beginning of the twenty-first century BC and Moses and the exodus at mid-fifteenth century BC. Many other Bible-believing scholars argue for dates about two centuries later. Since the traditional dates are widely used in time lines found in many study Bibles, we have opted for those dates. Nevertheless, it is important to recognize that the dates are disputed.

- *Dates of Jesus' birth and crucifixion*—The dates of the birth and death of Jesus are also subject to some debate. Cases have been made for birth dates ranging from 7–2 BC and dates for the crucifixion ranging from AD 26–36. For the purposes of this book, we use the widely accepted dates of 6–4 BC and AD 30, respectively.

WHAT *IS* GOD'S STORY?

It is a simple one. The Creator of all things decided to make human beings fundamentally different from any other creature. These humans would share so many of the attributes of the Creator that they could talk to the Creator . . . and talk *back* to the Creator . . . and even challenge the authority of the Creator!

And they did.

But two things happened. It is similar to what happens when members of a royal family mount an insurrection against a king and it fails. Humankind lost the ability to live like royalty, and soon they forgot what it was like to *be* royalty.

Instead of abandoning the rebels to their own devices, God began to implement a plan to restore the traitors to their original state. His first step was to create a nation that he would instruct to live as his children once again. By demonstrating that lifestyle (even imperfectly), this nation would show other nations how to live to the fullest.

Although these people learned how they *should* live, their rebellion against God kept them from fully living up to his standards. So another step was necessary. They needed to become royalty again; the penalty for their treason had to be paid. The only fair penalty was the life of the rebel. But how could one be restored if he or she were dead!

In his mercy God allowed them to offer a life as a token of their own. As harsh as requiring the lives of their best livestock sounds, it was a mere fraction of the real debt. These offerings were only a promise of a perfect substitute. God promised that a new prince, one who would fully model God's moral nature, would be born to them. This God-born prince came, led a perfect life . . . and then paid the death penalty that he did not owe!

Because of his justice, God restored the innocent one to life. The new prince, having paid the death penalty for humankind, invited them to share his nature. He gave them the power to more fully keep the rules and paid the debt they owed when they failed.

The prince placed these followers in a community consisting of men and women everywhere. This group would continue to invite others to accept the offer of the prince and join in this community until the day the prince would return to take his people to the perfect kingdom intended for them from the beginning.

But this is no mere story. It was played out in history, as you will see in the following pages.

Only God is eternal. Before anything was, God existed. Out of nothing (ex nihilo, as the philosophers and theologians say) came all the material of our universe through the animating energy of the Creator.

By design, all that exists came into being, one step at a time. At the apex of that

GOD CREATES

ITS PART IN GOD'S PLAN

Because a perfect Creator designed the universe, it was good in its original state. There were no design flaws requiring a factory recall. But out of love, God handed some supervisory authority over to humankind. This was not a mistake but part of a plan that actually predated creation.

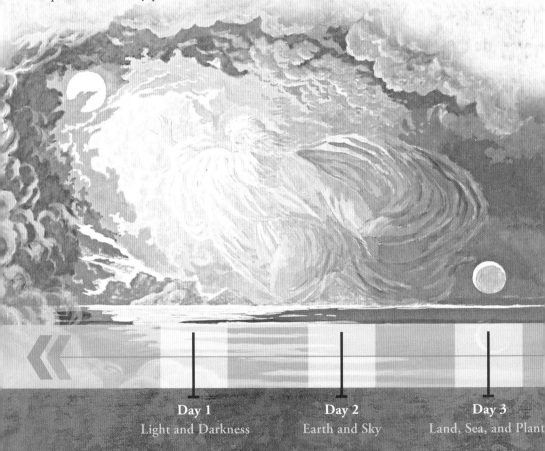

Day 1
Light and Darkness

Day 2
Earth and Sky

Day 3
Land, Sea, and Plant

The biblical account of creation is simply told and outlines an orderly work of God. Other creation stories differ greatly:

In the Bakuba (in Africa) creation story, the giant Mbombo vomited up the sun, moon, and stars.

process came the crown jewel of the universe. Human beings were not simply the last beings to come into existence. They were qualitatively different. Humans alone among creatures bear the likeness of God's nature. We were designed to know God and to serve as superintendents of all that he created.

EVERYTHING

When it happened...
Before recorded history

MAJOR THEMES

GOD IS SEPARATE FROM CREATION. Time itself had a beginning. Every atom of matter in this universe had a beginning. Only God stands outside of space, eternal and omnipresent. The universe does not contain God nor flow from God. God is not the collective breath of all living things. He is separate and totally "other."

ALL LIFE IS NOT CREATED EQUAL. Is swatting a mosquito murder? Is having a pet slavery? Is animal testing torture? The Bible is clear that all life is given value by virtue of creation and certainly should never be the victim of cruel treatment. But the Bible is also clear that God intended humans to be in charge of all creation, preserving it while at the same time using it for their benefit.

GOD HAS A SPECIAL PLAN FOR HUMANKIND. Human beings were created for relationship with God. God supplied the first humans with a special place, a special job in caring for that place, and special provisions for their health and safety.

DAILY READING PLAN

January 1: Genesis 1:1–2:3; Psalm 8
January 2: Job 38, 39
January 3: Job 40, 41

Day 4	**Day 5**	**Day 6**	**Day 7**
Heavenly Bodies	Birds and Fish	Land Animals and Humans	Rest

The ancient Finns (Finland) told of the universe being created when a giant egg was broken.

Raëlism, a modern religion created in the 1970s, teaches that space aliens created life on earth and the conditions necessary to support it.

At some point in time, God created spiritual messengers we know as angels. Apparently one angel rebelled against divine authority and brought others into battle with him. Those angels were defeated and cast out of Heaven. Later in the Bible we

ANGELS, DEMONS,

ITS PART IN GOD'S PLAN

The problem of evil is not an easy one to resolve. The Bible says little about the origin of Satan and demons, but certainly acknowledges their existence. All we can assume is that as destructive as evil is, God chose to allow for its possibility by giving created beings free will, even though they might then choose to reject goodness and God himself.

When it happened...
Before recorded history

DAILY READING PLAN
January 4: Isaiah 14:12-14; Ezekiel 28:12-19
January 5: Jude 6; Revelation 12:3, 4, 7-9
January 6: John 8:42-47

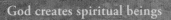

God creates spiritual beings

The Bible teaches that Satan is lower than God, is evil, and will be completely defeated. This view is sometimes different from mythological horned or mischievous beings.

Baphomet was a pagan goat god of the Middle Ages, revived by 19th-century Satanists.

learn more about the rebellious angel we know as the devil. He is commonly known for what he does. The title Satan *means "accuser" and "adversary."*

AND SATAN

MAJOR THEMES

A SPIRIT WORLD EXISTS. The supernatural world is just as real as the material world. Both contain conscious beings, and God created the inhabitants of both realms.

SATAN IS NOT GOD'S EQUAL. The world is not a battleground for two equal and opposite moral forces. The outcome of the battle between good and evil is not uncertain. Satan was created by God, is limited by God, and will be ultimately and completely defeated by God.

REBELLION AGAINST GOD IS THE SOURCE OF EVIL. Cold is the absence of heat. Darkness is the absence of light. Evil is the refusal to do good. When heat and light are removed, cold and darkness are left in their places. Evil is not created. It is simply the state of something or someone when goodness is removed. Some spiritual beings chose to turn from their appointed places and tried to take God's authority as their own. Throughout human history, power-hungry humans would imitate that sin of the devil and meet similar fates.

The devil and his angels rebel against God's authority

These defeated angels are called Satan and his demons

Yama of Eastern religions is often referred to as the first man who died, and then became the lord of death.

Loki is the Norse trickster god who makes trouble for all the other gods of Norse mythology.

After God created all the land animals, he created Adam. As God's appointed caretaker of creation, Adam was given the task of examining, categorizing, and naming all other creatures. In doing so, Adam found no other creature like himself. God then created the female of the human species to be the only perfect complement to Adam.

ADAM AND EVE

When it happened...
Before recorded history

God creates
animals

God creates Adam

References to Adam and Eve in the New Testament are made to substantiate important social truths:

Jesus taught that the God-ordained union of Adam and Eve signified that marriage is meant to be a lifetime commitment.

ITS PART IN GOD'S PLAN

God did more than create a mechanical universe. Life, especially human life, is more than the interaction of the chemicals that compose it. Humankind was not complete without relationships. Adam and Eve received provisions and direction from a loving Creator, but he also gave them one another to help, support, and love.

MAJOR THEMES

AMONG THE CREATED BEINGS, THERE ARE NONE EQUAL TO HUMANS. Although God created human life from the same chemical elements from which the rest of the universe is composed, only human life contains God's unique signature—his breath, his image. Those who use animal names to insult and objectify people should know that such labels are inaccurate. As Adam discovered when naming animals, they all differ greatly from humankind.

GOD CREATED MAN AND WOMAN TO COMPLETE EACH OTHER. Throughout the process of creation, God pronounced what he had made as being good. But upon looking at Adam without a companion, God saw that a solitary man was not good.

GOD CREATED MARRIAGE. It is significant that God created Eve by taking a part of Adam from him. In marriage the missing part is replaced, uniting a man and wife as "one flesh"—a single, complete unit.

Adam names the animals

God creates Eve

The apostle Paul taught that all nations have Adam as a common ancestor and that God wants people of every race and nation to come to know him.

God had only one prohibition in Eden: eating from one forbidden tree. The serpent, Satan, tempted Eve to imitate his sin and rebel against God's authority. Immediately after succumbing to temptation, Adam and Eve knew that they were separated from God and tried to hide in

ADAM AND EVE

ITS PART IN GOD'S PLAN

By willfully choosing to usurp God's authority, Adam and Eve declared war on their Creator. The results were devastating. But instead of totally destroying the beloved traitors, God began a course of action that would restore his relationship with human-kind. Yet even from the beginning, it was clear that reconciliation with a just God could only be obtained when a death penalty was paid.

MAJOR THEMES

GOD SAYS YES MORE THAN HE SAYS NO. Of all the trees in the Garden of Eden, including the tree of life that gave them eternal life, only one was forbidden. Adam and Eve did not sin because God gave them an impossible list of demands. They sinned because they wanted to be like God, free from any authority.

SIN DESTROYS EVERYTHING IT TOUCHES. When an electrical appliance is unplugged, that appliance is not just slowed or weakened—it is dead. When Adam and Eve chose to disconnect themselves from God, the results were equal-ly dramatic. Their relationship with God, their relationship with one another, and even their relationship with the natural world were totally changed.

ONLY GOD CAN COVER THE RESULTS OF SIN. Immediately after disobey-ing God, Adam and Eve had the urge to cover themselves in God's presence. They created garments out of leaves. God replaced their ineffectual attempt to cover themselves, with clothing made from animal skins. Animals had to die. The message was clear: The penalty for treason is death. But a merciful God would find a way to pay that price for the traitor.

God prohibits eating from
the tree of the knowledge of
good and evil

The serpent tempts Eve

shame. Their world changed radically after this treasonous act, and they were expelled from the paradise in which they once lived.

REBEL

DAILY READING PLAN

January 12: Genesis 3
January 13: Romans 1:18-32
January 14: Romans 5:1-11

When it happened...
Before recorded history

Adam and Eve
disobey God

God expels Adam
and Eve from Eden

In Greek mythology, Pandora opened a large jar ("box"), unleashing terrible things on humankind. Is this a mythologized version of Eve and the forbidden fruit?

The results of sin were immediate and ugly. In a fit of jealousy, Cain killed his younger brother and attempted to hide the crime from God. God sent Cain away from his presence. Normally this would have meant that the relatives of Abel would have sought out Cain

CAIN, ABEL, AND

ITS PART IN GOD'S PLAN

Cain may have been the first to try to approach God on his own terms, but he certainly was not the last. To this day individuals seek God through ways that seem best to them. These attempts are unsuccessful. And they continue to result in anger, hatred, and bloodshed.

DAILY READING PLAN
January 15: Genesis 4
January 16: Matthew 23:33-39
January 17: Hebrews 11:4; 12:24

God sets up a
sacrificial system

Cain and Abel offer
differing sacrifices

This story of the first murder has inspired fiction
writers past and present:

Pulitzer Prize–winning novel *East of Eden* by John Steinbeck
Recurring characters Cain and Abel in DC Comics and Vertigo graphic novels
British novel and TV miniseries *Kane and Abel*

and avenged Abel's death by killing him. But God mercifully spared Cain's life by placing his stamp of ownership on him. God gave Eve another son, Seth.

SETH

When it happened...
Before recorded history

MAJOR THEMES

GOD'S COVENANT IS NONNEGOTIABLE. Although the Bible does not specifically say so, it seems likely that God clearly taught Adam's family the necessity of animal sacrifice. Instead of using his goods to purchase a suitable sacrifice, Cain arrogantly felt that he could come to God on his own terms.

SIN IS PROGRESSIVE, ONE LEADING TO ANOTHER. Cain's arrogance led to anger. Cain's anger led to murder. There may be common sins or everyday sins, but there are no small sins. All sin is deadly.

GOD'S PLANS WILL NOT BE THWARTED. Although Cain refused to follow God and killed his brother who *had* obeyed God, God's work would continue through someone else—Seth, the ancestor of Noah.

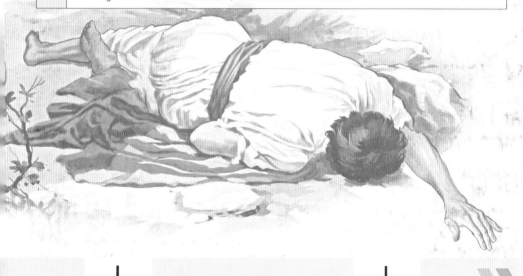

Cain kills Abel
and is punished

God gives Eve
another child

Rejecting God, humanity had sunk into complete decadence. God chose Noah to construct a barge (ark) that would contain the biological building blocks for a cleansed world. Noah built an ark to God's specifications,

NOAH AND

When it happened...
Before recorded history

ITS PART IN GOD'S PLAN

Adam and Eve got their wish—independence from God for themselves and for their descendants. But complete independence from God resulted in a human race totally devoid of redeeming value. God intervened in this downward spiral and chose Noah to be his agent to save the world from human beings seeking to be their own gods.

Humankind becomes completely corrupt

Noah builds the ark

Cultures all over the world have a story of a great flood, leading one to believe they all come from the memory of a single historical event. But unlike the Noah account, many are very fanciful:

According to a myth of aboriginal Australians, a frog drank all the water in the world, then caused a flood when other animals made him laugh.

God filled the boat with animals, and he preserved these voyagers through a cataclysmic deluge.

THE FLOOD

DAILY READING PLAN

MAJOR THEMES

THERE IS NO GOOD WITHOUT GOD. The ancient world before the great flood was evil beyond our imagination. Allowed to be free agents, unfettered by God's direction, humankind created a totally inhuman society. The further one runs from the heavenly, the more hellish life becomes.

IT IS POSSIBLE TO STAND AGAINST THE CROWD. Noah was not perfect. The Bible is very honest about his shortcomings. But Noah was willing to stand against the totally depraved moral climate of his day and to refuse to make himself the god of his own life.

GOD'S PRIMARY WORK IS SAVING, NOT DESTROYING. The emphasis of the account of Noah is not on God's wrath but on his mercy. God did not need to destroy the ancient world. Left on its own, humankind would surely have done that! It was saving the world, not destroying it, that required God's intervention. This act of mercy would foreshadow God's final plan for reaching into human history and offering shelter from destruction for all humankind.

God floods the earth

In Hindu mythology Vishnu, in the form of a fish, warned Manu of an impending flood. Manu built a boat, and he alone survived.

In Incan mythology, the creator god Viracocha sent a flood to destroy giants on the earth.

After the occupants of the ark disembarked, Noah offered a sacrifice to God. God made a personal peace treaty (covenant) with Noah and his descendants that spelled out two basic requirements of civilized society. God demanded

THE RAINBOW

DAILY READING PLAN

January 22: 2 Corinthians 1:18-22

January 23: Genesis 9:1-17

January 24: Psalm 19:1-6

January 25: Micah 6:8

Flood waters
subside

Noah and family
leave the ark

A rainbow may signify a promise
or a curse in cultures worldwide.

The common Irish legend
testifies to a pot of gold at
the end of the rainbow.

that humankind act as responsible caretakers of creation and value human life. He "signed" this treaty with the rainbow in the sky.

COVENANT

ITS PART IN GOD'S PLAN

Later when God made other covenants with people, those agreements would expand the commands of this treaty, not revoke them. The commands of Noah's covenant remain in effect today. Any culture interested in survival would be wise to take note.

When it happened...
Before recorded history

Where it happened...
The great flood ended, and the ark rested on the mountains of Ararat in modern-day Turkey.

MAJOR THEMES

GOD WANTS TO COMMUNICATE CLEARLY WITH HUMANKIND. After the experience of the great flood, surely the smallest rain shower could cause apprehension. The rainbow is a universal symbol of God's promise never again to destroy the world with water. God does not communicate in conspiratorial whispers to a few, but with larger-than-life images that can be understood by all.

WE ARE CALLED TO CARE FOR THE GOOD THINGS GOD GIVES. An irresponsible tenant does not maintain the property that he rents from the owner. In this covenant with all humankind, God calls us to rule over creation on his behalf. In doing so we neither destroy our surroundings for selfish gain nor allow them to fall into disarray due to our indifference.

HUMAN LIFE MUST BE RESPECTED AND PROTECTED. The importance of our being unique creatures fashioned in God's image is the cornerstone of civil law. Civilization cannot survive if human life is treated as a disposable commodity.

God makes a covenant with
Noah and his descendants

Bulgarian legends teach that one changes gender when passing under a rainbow.

In the mythology of ancient Slavs, a man touched by the rainbow is drawn to Heaven and becomes a demonic creature.

After getting off the ark, Noah's family began to repopulate the earth. On the plains of Shinar (Babylon, modern-day Iraq), human arrogance again reared its head. The men of that day attempted to build a temple tower so high that it reached the heavens. God

THE TOWER OF

ITS PART IN GOD'S PLAN

Even though God allowed humanity a do-over after the great flood, people continued to make the same self-destructive mistakes. The more human beings tried to be their own gods, the more godless, broken, and scattered they became.

DAILY READING PLAN

January 26: Genesis 11:1-9
January 27: Acts 17:24-31
January 28: Revelation 5:9, 10

MAJOR THEMES

JUST BECAUSE WE CAN DOESN'T MEAN WE SHOULD. In our day the growth of technology makes it possible to disobey God in ways only imagined before! After the flood the cutting-edge technology of brick baking and brick-laying made it possible to build towers of a height formerly impossible. But the fact that the people of that day tried to use technology to lessen their dependence on and obedience to God made their use of technology an offense against God. Technology alone is not the mark of advancement of a civilization.

SALVATION COMES FROM THE TOP DOWN, NOT BOTTOM UP. The tower of Babel was not merely a skyscraper. It was what is known as a ziggurat, a temple tower. Instead of worshiping God in the way they had been instructed, these people attempted to reach God in their own way and by their own merit. In contrast, the Bible teaches that we can only know God when he reaches down to us, not when we try to elevate ourselves to be noticed by him.

LACK OF COMMUNICATION BRINGS SEPARATION AND ISOLATION. When the people could not communicate with one another, they gathered with those they *could* understand and isolated themselves accordingly.

The descendants of Noah's sons —Shem, Ham, and Japheth— become all nations of the world

Post-flood humanity tries to reach God by building a temple tower to the heavens

World cultures have fanciful variations on the story of the tower of Babel:

An ancient Greek myth told that men had lived for ages without law under the rule of Zeus and spoke one language. The god Hermes brought diverse languages and, along with them, separation into nations—and war.

interrupted construction by taking away a common language and scattering the human population throughout the world.

BABEL

When it happened...
Before recorded history

Where it happened...
On the plains of Shinar
(in what is now Iraq)

God confuses the languages of these people,
scattering them all over the world

The Bantu people of East Africa told of a severe famine that caused madness, aimless wandering, and the jabbering of strange words.

A Hindu myth taught that people of the earth ate from a forbidden "proud tree." Brahma punished them by scattering them and confusing their languages.

Job was a wealthy man known for his reverence and morality. Suddenly Job's fortunes were lost, his family was destroyed, and his health failed. Unknown to anyone, the plight of Job was the result of God allowing Satan to test Job's beliefs with hardship. Job's friends came to comfort

JOB AND THE

ITS PART IN GOD'S PLAN

Even before recorded history, human beings struggled with the idea of the justice of God. The account of Job does not give simplistic answers to the questions. In fact, many of Job's words seem almost irreverent. Yet his story shows the results of humankind living in a spiritual war zone, and it holds the promise of a final resolution to this conflict.

Satan receives permission to test Job

Job meets financial and personal ruin

Job and his friends debate the reason for his suffering

The book of Job never minimizes the pain Job suffered, but also refuses to say that Job deserved his suffering. This differs from common beliefs about suffering:

Karma is the belief of Eastern religions that the suffering of a person is brought about by his actions.

him in his suffering, but ended up arguing that Job had somehow brought tragedy on himself. Finally, God intervened and gave Job even more than he had at first.

JUSTICE OF GOD

When it happened...
Before recorded history

Where it happened...
In the land of Uz, which may have been in what is now northwestern Saudi Arabia or southern Syria

DAILY READING PLAN
January 29: Job 2
January 30: Job 19
January 31: Job 42

MAJOR THEMES

BAD THINGS HAPPEN TO GOOD PEOPLE. Many problems come from poor choices. Yet because life also has a spiritual, invisible component, such is not always the case. Bad things happen to people who do bad things. Bad things happen to people in the proximity of people who do bad things. But bad things may happen to good people because of evil outside the natural world.

WE MAY NOT UNDERSTAND THE REASONS FOR TRAGIC EVENTS. When we or other people are experiencing pain, we want an explanation. We want to understand the reason for suffering. Job's friends pressed him to admit wrong-doing so that they could pinpoint the cause of his problems. Job cried to God himself to explain why his life was in turmoil. But in the end, no explanation was ever given.

DESPITE EVIL, GOD REMAINS ALL-POWERFUL AND LOVING. Righting the existence of pain with the idea of a loving, all-powerful God may seem difficult. Although we speak of "the patience of Job," during his time of suffering, Job was anything but patient! Yet Job learned that when one remains loyal to God, suffering is temporary. That suffering may end in this life or in the next, but for the children of God, the best days are always yet to come.

God restores Job

Chinese philosophy speaks of yin and yang. This is the belief that good and evil are necessary parts of the whole, that suffering is necessary for appreciating pleasure.

German philosopher Friedrich Nietzsche, noted for saying "God is dead," used the Latin phrase *amor fati* in relation to suffering. He saw suffering as a way to improve us, saying, "Whatever does not kill me makes me stronger."

God appeared to Abram and promised to make his family a mighty nation that would occupy the land of Canaan and would bring the blessings of God to all humankind. Abram and his wife Sarai and his nephew Lot left their homeland to travel to Canaan.

GOD FOUNDS A

When it happened...
2096–2091 BC

Where it happened...
Abram moved from his home in Ur (now Tell el-Mukayyar, Iraq) to Haran (in what is now the country of Turkey) and on to Canaan (Palestine).

2167 BC
Birth of Abram

2157 BC
Birth of Sarai

2500 BC or earlier
Silk industry begins in China

A couple of facts make this promise remarkable. First, Abram and Sarai were unable to have children, so it would appear that their family line would begin and end with them. Second, the land God showed Abram was already occupied.

NATION

DAILY READING PLAN

February 1: Genesis 11:27-32
February 2: Genesis 12:1-9
February 3: Acts 7:2-5; Hebrews 11:8-10
February 4: Genesis 12:10-20

ITS PART IN GOD'S PLAN

Human beings were so greatly separated from God that extreme measures were necessary to communicate to them. Even today, nations seem to advocate for a specific political philosophy. So it is logical that God would create a nation that was called to know, live by, and teach *his* message. From that nation would come the final king who would unite all humankind.

MAJOR THEMES

GOD DOES NOT NEED OUR HELP. There were mighty nations at the time of Abram. Why did God not find the strongest nation and choose it to be his mouthpiece to the world? Because God is fully capable of building his own nation from scratch! In this case, God would build a mighty nation from an infertile couple—evidence that the working out of his plan was all his doing.

BEING CHOSEN BY GOD IS A RESPONSIBILITY, NOT AN ENTITLEMENT. God built a chosen nation. But that did not mean that these people were especially worthy. Nor did it mean that God was choosing people to pamper like a doting grandfather would. Rather, the job of God's nation would be to help other nations know God's plan by their words and their actions.

GOD'S TIMING IS PERFECT. Nothing about this story makes sense from a human perspective! God chose an infertile couple and waited to give them children while their biological clocks were ticking. God promised to give his chosen family land, but that land was occupied. Yet when the time came, all would be ready.

2096 BC Abram, Sarai, and Lot begin their move from Ur to Haran to Canaan

2092 BC The Lord promises Abram that he will become a great nation and will occupy Canaan

2091 BC Abram, Sarai, and Lot migrate to Egypt because of a famine in Canaan, then return

c. 2100 BC Bronze tools begin to be used in Southeast Asia

ZERESHK

In Canaan, Abram and Lot became prosperous. Yet that prosperity caused conflicts between their households. Lot chose to move his household into the Jordan Valley and eventually into the morally reprehensible city of Sodom.

LOT AND SODOM

ITS PART IN GOD'S PLAN

The destruction of Sodom and Gomorrah cautions us that God will intervene with judgment before he allows the immorality of a city, state, or nation to corrupt the entire world. Even so, Lot's relatively brief interaction with Sodom's decadence had long-term results. Drunkenness and incest between Lot and his daughters produced two nations (Moab and Ammon) that would be a continuing source of problems for the descendants of Abram in the years to come.

MAJOR THEMES

MATERIAL WEALTH IS NOT ALWAYS A BLESSING. It might seem that God allowed Abram to be rewarded for deception when he left Egypt with more wealth. In fact, the wealth actually brought some disastrous consequences. Family infighting separated Lot from Abram and made Lot more vulnerable to the evil forces surrounding him.

ONE BAD CHOICE CAN LEAD TO OTHERS. Lot moved toward Sodom. Then he moved *into* Sodom. This caused Lot and his family to be taken as prisoners of war when Sodom's leaders became involved in an ill-advised conflict. Lot's family grew so accustomed to the immorality of Sodom that some of them were destroyed with the city.

GOD WANTS US TO PRAY FOR THE WELL-BEING OF OTHERS. Although Abram was physically separated from Lot and his household, Abram continued to show concern for his nephew. Abram gathered an army to free Lot and other citizens of Sodom who were captured in battle. Even more significantly, Abram pleaded with God to save Lot when God destroyed Sodom.

2091 BC Households of Abram and Lot separate due to property disputes. Lot and his household become prisoners of war.

2134 BC Collapse of Egypt's Old Kingdom

As a result of Lot's choices, he was taken captive in a war, escaped only by God's intervention when Sodom was destroyed, and lost family members, including his wife.

When it happened...
2091–2068 BC

Where it happened...
Lot and his household moved into the Jordan Valley and eventually into the city of Sodom.

From 2068 BC God destroys Sodom and Gomorrah. Lot and his daughters become the ancestors of the nations of Moab and Ammon.

2040 BC Mentuhotep restores centralized government in Egypt, marking the beginning of the Middle Kingdom

Concerned that they were growing old but remained childless, Abram and Sarai tried to fulfill God's promise for a child in their own way. In accordance with the customs of Canaan, Sarai offered her Egyptian servant Hagar as a surrogate spouse.

HAGAR AND

ITS PART IN GOD'S PLAN

The man we call Abraham is a revered figure in three major world religions—Judaism, Christianity, and Islam. Yet the Bible is brutally honest about his mistakes. Despite those mistakes, however, God's plan would not be thwarted. In his time God would fulfill his promise to Abram.

MAJOR THEMES

HUMAN BEINGS ARE NOT QUALIFIED TO DO GOD'S JOB. Sarai and Abram grew impatient for God to keep his promise to provide an heir. That was a big mistake. The attempt to do God's will their way led to the birth of Ishmael, the ancestor of the Arab nations. Sarai and Abram's arrogance began a conflict which plays out daily in the Middle East to this day.

GOD SIDES WITH PEOPLE WHO ARE OPPRESSED. Even though God would have a special relationship with Abram and his heirs, that relationship did not give Abram license to mistreat others. God was quick to hear the cries of Hagar and come to her aid.

SOCIETY'S RULES ARE NOT NECESSARILY GOD'S RULES. In ancient Canaan, polygamy was acceptable. Involuntary servitude—slavery—was routinely practiced. A wealthy landowner could have a sexual relationship with a female servant, and no one would object. But that does not mean that those acts sanctioned by society would not lead to unpleasant results!

When it happened...
2082–2066 BC

Where it happened...
Canaan and its desert lands

2091 BC Abram and Sarai bring servants from Egypt back to Canaan

2500 BC Hittites establish empire in Anatolia (modern Turkey)

DYNAMOSQUITO

c. 2100 BC Great Ziggurat (temple) of Ur (near Nasiriyah, Iraq) constructed

After Hagar conceived, Sarai responded with jealousy, which drove her pregnant servant into the desert. Hagar would later return and give birth to Ishmael. Eventually, though, both mother and child would be driven into the desert.

ISHMAEL

DAILY READING PLAN

February 9: Genesis 15
February 10: Genesis 16; 21:8-21
February 11: Genesis 17

2082 BC Sarai gives Hagar to Abram to be a surrogate mother to their heir and then causes a pregnant Hagar to run away

2068 BC God changes the names of Abram and Sarai to Abraham and Sarah

2066 BC Sarah insists that Abraham send both Hagar and her son Ishmael away

Thirteen years after Abram's misguided plan to fulfill God's promise of an heir, God acted. God appeared to Abram and identified himself as El Shaddai (literally, "God is enough"). God also changed the name of Abram (meaning "exalted father") to Abraham ("father of many") and the name of Sarai (possibly meaning "contentious") to Sarah ("princess"). God gave the yet-to-be-born son the name Isaac ("he laughs"). Furthermore,

BIRTH OF ISAAC

DAILY READING PLAN
February 12: Genesis 18:1-15
February 13: Genesis 20
February 14: Genesis 21:1-7

2068 BC God institutes the sign of circumcision

2068 BC Three visitors promise Abraham and Sarah a son

2068 BC Abraham pleads for Lot and Sodom

c. 2200 BC Dogs, goats, pigs, oxen, and sheep domesticated in China

God instituted the practice of circumcision as a physical sign of the agreement between him and Abraham and his descendants. Afterwards, three angelic messengers came to Abraham and Sarah and repeated the news of Isaac's impending birth. The very mention of a nearly hundred-year-old man fathering a child with a woman almost as old caused the reaction for which Isaac would be named—laughter.

ITS PART IN GOD'S PLAN

Isaac was not just Abraham and Sarah's son. Because of divine intervention, he was in a real sense God's son. As such, he would point to another who would have that title in the distant future.

MAJOR THEMES

GOD IS ENOUGH. To this day when Jewish parents have had enough of the noisiness of their children, they might say in Hebrew: *"Dai, dai!"* which means "Enough, enough!" After Abram and Sarai tried to fulfill God's promise of an heir in their own way, God said the same thing! God referred to himself as El Shaddai. God is the source of all life and nourishment and is able to provide everything to those who love him.

GOD'S RELATIONSHIP WITH HIS PEOPLE IS ALL-ENCOMPASSING AND INTIMATE. Throughout the centuries people have tried to devise an outward mark that would speak of their holiness. Those have included a certain hairstyle, a type of clothing, or symbolic jewelry. When God chose a way to mark his people, he chose a mark that was incredibly personal. It was also a constant reminder that God has authority over even the most private areas of our lives.

DON'T LAUGH AT GOD . . . LAUGH *WITH* HIM! Following God is often thought of as a somber and humorless affair. Nothing could be further from the truth! When God overcomes the limitations of humankind by his remarkable provisions, it is a reason to celebrate.

When it happened...
2068–2067 BC

Where it happened...
Abraham and Sarah were living near the great trees of Mamre.

2067 BC Abraham and Sarah travel to Negev (south of Canaan) and return

2067 BC A son is born to Sarah and is named Isaac ("he laughs")

c. 2000 BC Horses domesticated in China

Years after Isaac was given to Abraham and Sarah, God tested Abraham by commanding Abraham to give his son back. In what appears to be a heartless demand, God told Abraham to sacrifice Isaac—on a mountain that would later be the home of the Jewish temple.

ABRAHAM IS

ITS PART IN GOD'S PLAN

As strange as this account appears to the modern mind, it is extremely important. The picture of an only son carrying wood on which he is to be sacrificed and walking up the side of a hill would be seen in all its fullness centuries later.

When it happened...
Sometime between 2055–2045 BC

Where it happened...
Abraham and Isaac took a three-day journey from their base camp to Mount Moriah, outside what would become the city of Jerusalem.

Sometime between 2066–2060 BC Abraham negotiates a peace treaty with the Philistines

2071 BC The first recorded battle in Ireland is said to have taken place on Magh Ithe (the Plain of Ithe)

As outrageous as this demand may have seemed, Abraham complied immediately. God stopped Abraham from going through with the sacrifice and provided an animal to be sacrificed in Isaac's place.

TESTED

DAILY READING PLAN

February 15: Genesis 22:1-19

February 16: Hebrews 11:17-19; 1 John 4:7-18

MAJOR THEMES

GOD IS DIFFERENT FROM FALSE GODS IN BOTH DEGREE AND DISPOSITION. The followers of pagan religions of Abraham's day asked their gods to increase the production of their fields and of their animals. Because of the miracle of Isaac, Abraham learned that the magnitude of God's power was far greater than any pagan fertility god! But Abraham knew that fertility gods often required worshipers to give back what they were given. Now Abraham would learn that God not only was a bigger giver than false gods but also would not capriciously take back what he had granted.

LOVE DEMANDS SACRIFICE. How consistent that the first time the word *love* is used in the Bible, it is used in the context of someone giving up his only son!

GOD IS A GIVER, NOT A TAKER. God owes us nothing. From the time of Adam and Eve, humankind has been actively in rebellion against God. And as is true in almost all human codes of justice, the penalty for treason is death. But God, in his generous nature, has always sought to provide a substitute that would take the death penalty from us.

Sometime between 2055–2045 BC Abraham acts to offer Isaac to God

2030 BC Sarah dies and is buried in Canaan

c. 2000 BC Farmers and herders travel south from Ethiopia and settle in Kenya

Isaac had twin sons, Esau and Jacob. Growing up, Jacob lived up to the meaning of his name —"devious one." Twice Jacob tricked Esau out of his inheritance, finally driving Esau into a murderous rage. After living and raising a family in exile, Jacob prepared to make amends with Esau. The night before that meeting, an angel of God wrestled with Jacob and changed his name to

JACOB'S NEW

ITS PART IN GOD'S PLAN

Throughout the rest of the Bible, the one true God is referred to as "the God of Abraham, Isaac, and Jacob." Jacob's twelve sons became the patriarchs of the twelve tribes of Israel.

MAJOR THEMES

GOD CAN USE SCOUNDRELS. Jacob always had an angle. Whether he was looking for a way to con the blessings of being a firstborn child from his older (though by minutes) twin brother or getting out of town without being stopped by his father-in-law, Jacob always seemed to be an unlikely head of God's nation. But to this day Jews trace their lineage back to him.

GOD CAN CHANGE SCOUNDRELS. Jacob would not be the last person who would have a life-changing encounter with God. As with others who would come later, change came with struggle and pain—but it came nonetheless.

WE NEED TO REMEMBER OUR VICTORIES AND LIMITATIONS. As strange as a wrestling match with an angel sounds, the results make a lot of sense. With a new name given by God, Jacob was able to celebrate a life of victory. Yet in the struggle Jacob suffered an injury that would remind him for the rest of his life of his dependence on God.

2027 BC Isaac marries Rebekah

2007 BC Rebekah bears twins, Esau and Jacob

Sometime between 1985–1980 BC Esau sells his rights as firstborn to Jacob for a meal

CAVORITE

c. 2000 BC Minoan palace civilization emerges on the island of Crete

Israel—*"the one who wrestles with God."*
It is under that new name that we
know the descendants of his twelve sons.
They became the nation of Israel.

DAILY READING PLAN

February 17: Genesis 24
February 18: Genesis 25:19-34; 27:1-40
February 19: Genesis 28:10-22; 32:22-32

NAME

When it happened...
1910 BC

Where it happened...
Jacob left Haran and prepared to
meet his estranged brother Esau
in eastern Canaan.

1930 BC Jacob has
a dream of a ladder
(ziggurat) to Heaven

1910 BC Jacob wrestles with an
angel as he travels to reconcile
with Esau

Jacob favored Joseph above his other eleven sons and gave him a special coat that may have marked him as the chief heir. Envious, Joseph's brothers sold him to traders who were descendants of Abraham's son Ishmael. These traders went to Egypt, the country of Ishmael's mother's

JOSEPH SUFFERS

DAILY READING PLAN
February 20: Genesis 37
February 21: Genesis 39
February 22: Genesis 40

1923–1910 BC Jacob fathers 12 sons and a daughter through his two wives and their maidservants

1899 BC Joseph's older brothers sell him into slavery. Potiphar of Egypt purchases Joseph.

ROSEMANIAKOS

c. 2000 BC Glass first produced in Syria, Mesopotamia, and Egypt

birth, and sold Joseph there. Because God was with Joseph, he survived and thrived in hostile conditions. Although a slave, he rose in rank to be the chief servant of his master. After being falsely accused of rape and imprisoned, Joseph became the trusted assistant to the warden.

ITS PART IN GOD'S PLAN

Biblical heroes are unflinchingly human. Jacob favored one son over the others, feeding conflict within his family. The envy of Joseph's brothers led to rage and attempted murder. Yet these incredibly flawed individuals became the honored founders of the nation of Israel.

When it happened...
1899–1886 BC

Where it happened...
Jacob and his sons settled in Canaan. Jacob's sons sold their brother Joseph into slavery, and he was taken to Egypt.

MAJOR THEMES

GOD IS PRESENT DURING BOTH GOOD TIMES AND BAD. Joseph went from being chief heir of a wealthy man to being slave of the chief servant of an influential leader to being a prisoner. Though Joseph's situation changed, at no time was he outside God's presence.

ACKNOWLEDGING GOD'S PRESENCE LEADS TO ETHICAL BEHAVIOR. Awareness of God's presence was the key to Joseph's integrity. Even when it appeared that he could do wrong secretly, he recognized that he could hide nothing from an all-knowing God.

GOD REMAINS TRUE THOUGH OTHERS DO NOT. Time and time again Joseph experienced betrayal. His own brothers plotted against him. The wife of his master accused him falsely. People who made promises to him failed to keep those promises. Yet such betrayal could not derail God's plans for Joseph.

Sometime between 1898–1891 BC Potiphar imprisons Joseph because of allegations of rape

1888 BC While in prison, Joseph interprets dreams of Pharaoh's baker and cupbearer

1886 BC Joseph released from prison

God remained with Joseph in prison. When told of troubling dreams of Pharaoh's imprisoned cupbearer (butler) and baker, Joseph revealed their fates by the power of God. Although the cupbearer promised Joseph he would try to secure his release after he himself was restored to Pharaoh's good graces, he failed to do so.

JOSEPH RULES

When it happened...
1886–1806 BC

Where it happened...
Joseph moved from an Egyptian prison to a high position in the Egyptian government. He and his reunited family would settle in Goshen in northern Egypt.

DAILY READING PLAN
February 23: Genesis 41
February 24: Genesis 42, 43
February 25: Genesis 44, 45

1886 BC Joseph made governor of Egypt

1878–1877 BC Joseph's brothers go to Egypt to buy grain. Joseph reveals his identity. Jacob and family move to Egypt.

c. 2000 BC Pre-Classic period of the Mayan civilization in Mesoamerica begins

Two years later when Pharaoh had disturbing dreams, the cupbearer remembered Joseph and recommended that he be asked to interpret them. Joseph recognized the dreams as God revealing that Egypt would have seven years of bumper crops followed by seven years of famine. Pharaoh then appointed Joseph as prime minister in charge of preparing for the famine and administering food during it.

The predicted famine was widespread, even affecting the land of Joseph's family. Jacob sent his sons to Egypt to obtain grain. While the reunion of Joseph with his brothers was as dramatic as would be expected, Joseph assured them that he held no grudges and would seek no vengeance. The entire tribe of Jacob relocated to Egypt, where they were given land and prospered for the following few centuries.

ITS PART IN GOD'S PLAN

God had told Abram years before that his descendants would have to spend four hundred years in a foreign nation before taking possession of the promised land of Canaan. The reason for this was that the Canaanite society had not yet become totally depraved and worthy of judgment. The stay in Egypt would also later serve as a reminder to show kindness to foreigners in their own land.

MAJOR THEMES

GOD WANTS US TO KNOW HIS PLANS FOR US. The Bible presents the picture of a God who has both a plan and the power to implement it. Furthermore, God loves humankind and does not want us to be ignorant of what he wants *for* us and *from* us.

LIFE IS HARD, BUT GOD IS GOOD. Even though he was the favored son of a wealthy man, Joseph did not have an easy life. God's presence did not guarantee a trouble-free life, but rather a life of meaning and purpose.

EVEN ACTIONS INTENDED FOR EVIL CAN BE USED BY GOD. Joseph refused to live in bitterness and resentment. While he was victimized time after time, he refused to play the role of a victim. His trust that God was in control kept him from despair and allowed him to live a life of ultimate victory.

1860 BC Jacob dies in Egypt and is buried in Canaan

1806 BC Joseph dies in Egypt

Woolly mammoth 32 USA

c. 1700 BC The last species of mammoth becomes extinct near the Arctic Circle

Though Jacob and his family were welcomed into Egypt during Joseph's rule, the political climate changed greatly in the following centuries. Because the Israelite population grew in number, the Egyptians were concerned about the security threat caused by the large

BIRTH OF MOSES

When it happened...
1526 BC

Where it happened...
Goshen in the Nile Delta of Egypt

DAILY READING PLAN
February 26: Exodus 1:1-14
February 27: Exodus 1:15–2:10
February 28/29: Acts 7:17-22;
Hebrews 11:22, 23

1806 BC
Death of Joseph

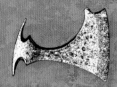

c. 1800 BC Iron Age
begins in India, Bronze
Age in Scandinavia

RAVICHANDAR

c. 1700–1650 BC Spread
of two-wheeled war
chariot in Middle East

number of foreigners in their land. For that reason they enslaved the people of Israel and actually ordered the extermination of any male child born to an Israelite family.

When a godly Israelite woman named Jochebed gave birth to a son, she hid him from the authorities. When that was no longer possible, she waterproofed a basket and placed her son in it among the reeds of the Nile River. The Pharaoh's daughter found the baby, named him Moses, and adopted him as a part of the royal family.

ITS PART IN GOD'S PLAN

The most powerful nation on earth wanted Moses dead at birth! Yet God not only spared his life but also allowed Moses to receive the upbringing of a prince. This prince of Egypt, however, would accept a far greater calling and become one of the key figures in biblical history.

MAJOR THEMES

NATIONS CHANGE, BUT GOD'S PLAN IS NEVER THWARTED. At one time the descendants of Israel were VIPs in Egypt. But the political winds shifted greatly, and Egypt began to see the Israelites as a threat to their national security. Certainly the Jews would have longed for the good old days when they and their faith in God were tolerated in Egypt. But whether or not God's people are in a position of political influence or not is largely irrelevant. God alone is sufficient to see that what he wants is accomplished.

GOD CHOOSES UNLIKELY CANDIDATES TO FULFILL HIS PURPOSES. It would have been easy to forget that Joseph first came to Egypt as a slave. Yet through God's power he rose to his position of influence. In the case of Moses, God would later allow a prince to go back into slavery! Either way, it is less about the human element and totally about the divine.

TAKING RISKS TO DO WHAT GOD WANTS WILL BE REWARDED. The arrogance of Pharaoh to order the execution of newborns was outrageous. Totally powerless people resisted his inhumane decree. Hebrew midwives, when called on to murder babies that they had just delivered, were ruled by their consciences, not the law of the land. Jochebed and her daughter Miriam attempted to hide a crying infant from civil authority at risk to their own lives. Yet all who risked to do right were rewarded.

1526 BC
Moses is born and adopted

c. 1600 BC Early alphabet invented by Canaanites

c. 1500 BC Rabbit domesticated in Europe

As a child and young man, Moses was known as the grandson of the Pharaoh. Yet his anger at the inequity between his life of royalty and the slavery of his own people continued to fester within him. This rage came to a head one day when he witnessed an

MOSES IS CALLED BY GOD

When it happened...
1486–1446 BC

Where it happened...
Midian, the land of the son of Abraham and his second wife Keturah

DAILY READING PLAN
March 1: Exodus 2:11-25
March 2: Exodus 3
March 3: Exodus 4:1-17

1486 BC Moses commits murder and flees to Midian, meets his future wife Zipporah

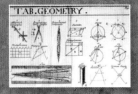

c. 1500 BC Geometry developed in Egypt

c. 1490 BC Cranaus, legendary king of Athens, deposed

Egyptian taskmaster beating a Hebrew slave. Moses killed the Egyptian and buried his body, thinking the murder would go unnoticed.

Moses soon discovered that his crime had been exposed and his adopted royal family sought to kill him. At the age of forty, he fled to Midian. During his decades in Midian, Moses married Zipporah and tended his father-in-law's flocks. It was then God confronted him from a burning bush.

From the ever-burning-yet-ever-living bush, God called Moses to be the kind of prince he was born to be—the kind that provides for rather than exploits his subjects. When Moses balked at parts of his assignment, God gave those duties to Moses' brother Aaron.

ITS PART IN GOD'S PLAN

Because humankind was so separated from God, being reintroduced to him was no easy task. God would reveal his nature in stages over centuries. Abraham, Isaac, and Jacob learned to know God as their provider. Through Moses God would reveal himself to be their rescuer as well.

MAJOR THEMES

DON'T GET TOO COMFORTABLE. Sometimes life at the top crashes to the bottom. It did so with Job, who in his depression prayed that he might die (Job 6:8, 9). We see this repeated in the life of Joseph. One minute he was the favored son of a wealthy man; the next, he was thrown into a pit! Likewise, almost instantly, Moses went from the company of royalty to the company of sheep. But in all cases, God remained in control.

GOD MAKES THE ORDINARY EXTRAORDINARY. Moses balked at the call to be God's representative confronting one of the most powerful nations on earth. Was a burned-out prince who had been reduced to caring for sheep for half of his life qualified for such a role? Of course not. That was the point. God illustrated what happens when he empowers the ordinary, by using Moses' own hand and a shepherd's rod as tools of his might.

GOD HAS A PERSONAL NAME. One of the first things we learn about a person is his or her name. Abraham, Isaac, and Jacob knew God only by his title, God Almighty. But from the time of Moses on, God's people would be on a first-name basis with him.

1446 BC Moses and the burning bush

CLAIRE H

c. 1400 BC Bronze helmets used in Crete

Moses and Aaron went to Pharaoh as God directed. But instead of freeing the Israelites, Pharaoh only made their slavery more severe. This was more than an act of arrogance; it was a challenge. The thought of one true God raised the hackles of

BATTLE AGAINST

When it happened...
1446 BC

Where it happened...
Goshen in the Nile Delta of Egypt

MAJOR THEMES

OUR ATTEMPT TO BE GODS ONLY MAKES OUR SITUATIONS WORSE. It would seem that Adam and Eve had provided enough evidence of that. But humankind refuses to learn! Consider the foolish display of the Egyptian magicians. Through Moses, God made the waters of the Nile undrinkable. In response, the magicians took the stored drinking water of the palace and fouled it as well! God brought about plagues of frogs and gnats, so the magicians "proved" their power by adding to rather than correcting the situation. Finally, God restrained their abilities and kept them from completely destroying themselves!

THE POWER OF GOD WILL EITHER PRODUCE WORSHIP OR REJECTION. The same sunlight that melts butter hardens clay. Likewise, the exhibition of God's power in the plagues could have caused Pharaoh's heart to melt. He could have admitted his error and worshiped the God of Israel. But Pharaoh recognized that submitting to God's authority meant relinquishing his own. So he allowed the acts of power to harden his heart, making him even more resistant to God.

GOD'S ULTIMATE ACT OF POWER FREES US FROM THE CONSEQUENCES OF OUR REBELLION. What humankind must do is surrender. From the beginning, God arranged that surrender would be shown by sacrifice. God authorized the penitent to offer a life in the place of their own as a sign of submission. Death passed over the households of Israel that were marked with the blood of a sacrificed lamb. Remembering how death passed over them in their escape from Egypt would become the yearly Passover festival practiced by Jews to this day.

1446 BC 10 plagues sent upon Egypt, each showing God's superiority to an Egyptian god

The Plagues
1. Water into blood: God vs. Hapi—god of the Nile
2. Frogs: God vs. Heket—goddess of fertility, water, and renewal
3. Gnats from the earth: God vs. Geb—god of the earth
4. Flies (a plague the magicians could not recreate): God vs. Khepri—god of creation and rebirth
5. Death of cattle: God vs. Hathor—goddess of love and protection

Pharaoh. Egypt was protected by ten gods, of which Pharaoh himself was chief. Pharaoh was willing to prove that those gods were sufficient. God took the challenge by directing Moses to demonstrate the superiority of the God of Israel over all ten gods, one by one.

EGYPTIAN GODS

DAILY READING PLAN

March 4: Exodus 7, 8
March 5: Exodus 9, 10
March 6: Exodus 11; 12:1-30

ITS PART IN GOD'S PLAN

In calling Abram, God had told him that his descendants would spend four hundred years in Egypt before taking possession of the land of promise. This served at least two purposes. It allowed God to illustrate his ability to save and lead out of bondage in the most dramatic of ways. It also gave the people of Canaan an opportunity to turn from their inhuman practices and not sink into the same moral depravity of the world before the flood of Noah.

6. Boils: God vs. Isis—goddess of medicine and health
7. Hail: God vs. Nut—goddess of the sky
8. Locusts from the sky: God vs. Seth—god of storms and destruction
9. Three days of darkness: God vs. Ra—god of the sun
10. Death of the firstborn: God vs. Pharaoh—ruling god over Egypt

The last of the ten plagues was leveled against the god-claims of Pharaoh.
By taking Pharaoh's firstborn son, God took away Pharaoh's heir to the throne.
Though Pharaoh at first allowed the Israelites to go, he quickly changed his
mind and sent his army to cut them off at the sea. But God rescued his people by
providing a path through the water. As was true in the days of Noah, God saved

EXODUS FROM

When it happened...
1446 BC

Where it happened...
Goshen in the Nile Delta of Egypt and the Sinai Peninsula

MAJOR THEMES

GOD DOES NOT LEAD HIS PEOPLE INTO DEAD-END STREETS. As one would expect of the army of a great empire, Pharaoh's generals were brilliant tacticians. They drove their fleeing slaves into a trap, bounded by water on one side and an army on the other. But they failed to grasp that the sea was God's creation that he could manipulate as he pleased. No obstacle is insurmountable for those who dare to be led by the Creator of all.

A GOD WHO SPECIALIZES IN JUDGMENT IS A FRIGHTENING THOUGHT. The idea that God punishes sinners sounds attractive until we realize that we are among that number! The spectacle of Pharaoh's army drowning in the sea caused celebration. Yet a sobering thought soon struck the people of Israel. *What if we anger God? Do we have any reason to believe we will not be destroyed?* The message of the Bible is that love, not judgment, is the primary characteristic of God. Judgment is a necessity born of the need to save those he loves.

SOMETIMES THE ONLY LOGICAL WAY TO REACT TO GOD IS WITH COMPLETE ASTONISHMENT. In order to feed his people, God created a food that never existed before and has not existed since. For six days a week, the Israelites would awaken to find a breadlike substance covering the ground surrounding them. This food they called manna could be prepared in a variety of ways and provided for all their nutritional needs. The name—meaning "What is it?"—showed the Israelites' utter amazement at the saving work of God.

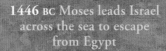

1446 BC Moses leads Israel across the sea to escape from Egypt

From c. 1450 BC Brahma worship in India

c. 1440 BC First metalworking in South America

his people from the water that proved to be the doom of those who challenged him.

After crossing the sea, the Israelites broke into songs of celebration. But then reality set in. How would a nation survive in a desert? Yet God was faithful by providing water and actually scheduling regular food deliveries to them!

EGYPT

DAILY READING PLAN
March 7: Exodus 12:31-51; 13
March 8: Exodus 14
March 9: Exodus 15, 16

ITS PART IN GOD'S PLAN

The most famous slave uprising in history is also the most unusual. The people of Israel did not bear a weapon against the Egyptians, but thoroughly trounced an empire's army. The slaves left captivity, not as paupers but with silver, gold, and the finest clothing given to them by a fearful populace. The leader of the escape was not a brash young general, but an eighty-year-old retired shepherd whose greatest asset was an unwavering faith in an all-powerful God.

c. 1400 BC Maize (corn) cultivated in Mesoamerica

God the Provider gave the Israelites wealth and daily food. God the Liberator opened the sea and allowed them to pass through. God the Guide led them with a pillar of cloud by day and a pillar of fire by night. But it was then time for the Israelites to meet God the Holy One.

GOD'S LAW FOR

When it happened...
1446 BC

Where it happened...
The Sinai Peninsula

ITS PART IN GOD'S PLAN

Our loved ones show their desire for a close relationship by giving us a photo to place on our mantel, in a locket, or in a wallet. People seeking that type of intimacy with a god have always created their own icons that would symbolize that god's presence. Such a practice was forbidden for God's people. God gave them a much more accurate image to pass from generation to generation—the book of the Law.

1446 BC God gives the Law on Mt. Sinai

c. 1790 BC Code of Hammurabi composed in Babylon

c. 1500 BC The Rig Veda (a collection of Hindu hymns) composed

Three months after leaving Egypt, Israel camped before a mountain in the Sinai Desert. From that mountain God would give the descendants of Abraham an unheard-of gift. In the past, men like Job struggled to know what God wanted of them. In giving the Law to the Israelites, God literally answered the question in writing.

ISRAEL

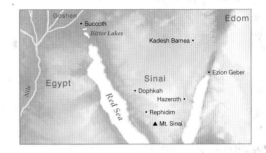

DAILY READING PLAN

March 10: Exodus 19

March 11: Exodus 20

March 12: Deuteronomy 5

MAJOR THEMES

GOD WANTS HIS PEOPLE TO SHARE THE RICHNESS OF HIS NATURE. To be holy simply means to have a separate nature. It would be unheard of for a king to want every member of his kingdom to be as royal as he was. But this was the call of the true king of Israel. God had created Adam and Eve to share his image. Yet the first couple squandered that gift. Giving the Law was a first step in restoring holiness to humankind. God would paint a clear picture of what holiness looked like and how it was to be lived out in this world.

GOD'S LAW IS NOT A LIST OF RULES BUT A PRACTICAL DESCRIPTION OF HIS NATURE. The Law of Moses was not a formula, but a portrait. The Law given on Sinai reflected who God was and, therefore, how he would govern as the king of a nation. Rather than an arbitrary list of dos and don'ts, the Law was a unique plan for living for those who would reflect God's holiness.

THE DISTINCTION BETWEEN SACRED AND SECULAR IS A FALSE ONE. Humankind has always made separate rules for living in God's presence and for living outside God's presence. This idea is incompatible with the idea of an omnipresent God! The Law of Moses was much more than the Ten Commandments. It was a detailed criminal code that covered specific penalties for infractions, a civil code mandating social norms, and even a public health code that taught how to eat properly and avoid exposure to disease. Every aspect of life is sacred, not just those actions dedicated to religious rites.

c. 622 BC Draconian Law in Athens

c. 500 BC Wisdom of Confucius in China

The Law came with a construction project attached. The nation of Israel was a nation whose king was God himself. Therefore, the Law gave a blueprint for building his quarters—the tabernacle.

Although it was God's desire for all his people to share his presence, the Law only

THE TABERNACLE

ITS PART IN GOD'S PLAN

The tabernacle testified to the presence of God among his people. As the Israelites traveled to Canaan, they set it up every time they settled and took it down every time they broke camp. Eventually the furnishings of the tabernacle, including the ark of the covenant, would rest in the temple in the capital city of their nation.

When it happened...
1446–1445 BC

Where it happened...
The Sinai Peninsula

DAILY READING PLAN
March 13: Exodus 36, 37
March 14: Exodus 38, 39
March 15: Leviticus 10

2091 BC Abram pays tithe to Melchizedek, king of Salem

1446 BC Gifts solicited from among the Israelites for the tabernacle

1446–1445 BC Construction of the tabernacle

served to reveal a problem: no one was worthy to enter the presence of God. So the Law also identified the intermediaries and outlined the regulations for them. Aaron and his descendants would be the only members of the nation able to approach God and offer sacrifices for the people.

AND THE
PRIESTHOOD

MAJOR THEMES

KNOWLEDGE OF GOD IS NOT ENOUGH. If a pilot's plane were to crash in the middle of a deep jungle, he would have two problems. He would not know where he was, and he would have lost the ability to fly. Therefore, a map alone would not solve his problem. Humankind "crashed" when Adam and Eve rebelled against God, giving them two problems. First, as generations passed they could no longer grasp the holiness of God to know how lost they were. Second, they so tarnished the image of God within them that they no longer had the ability to conform to the holiness of God even when they knew it. Therefore, along with the "map" of the Law, God began to rebuild their "plane" with a sacrificial system that constantly pointed out the deadly results when they failed to mirror God's holy nature.

MERCY IS THE CENTERPIECE OF GOD'S PLANS FOR US. In the middle of the tabernacle stood the ark of the covenant, the holiest place in this holy place. The top of the ark was known as the mercy seat, or place of covering. Thinking of the tabernacle as God's residence, his plan for restoring humanity to its original state sat squarely in the center of his dining room table!

PLAYING WITH RELIGION IS A DANGEROUS GAME. The business of paying for wrongdoing by offering sacrifices was a serious one. In a heartbreaking incident, Aaron's own sons, Nadab and Abihu, took their duties as priests lightly and did not follow the prescribed practices. As a result, they died in the very sacrificial flames they tried to manipulate.

1445 BC Death of
Nadab and Abihu

1129–1077 BC Amenhotep, high
priest of the Egyptian god Amun

c. 700 BC King Numa
appoints the leaping priests
(the Salii) of the god Mars

The journey from Egypt to Canaan was marred by complaints, disobedience, and outright treason. Even while Moses was still on Sinai receiving revelation from God, the people convinced Aaron to create an idol for them to worship. As the trip progressed, Moses' authority was continually challenged. Even Moses' own brother and sister questioned his ability to lead! After God had led them to the cusp of the promised land, they refused to enter, making plans to return to slavery in Egypt.

DISOBEDIENCE AND CONSEQUENCES

MAJOR THEMES

THE EASY WAY IS THE HARD WAY. God commanded Moses to compose a scouting party of one man from the lineage of each son of Jacob. The twelve spies entered into Canaan and brought back reports of a rich land occupied by formidable enemies. Ten of the twelve spies, despite the power of God they had witnessed in Egypt and thereafter, advised against entering the land. The people rebelled and even plotted to execute Moses, Aaron, and the two spies who sided with them. Although God did not allow them to follow through, their choice to avoid confrontation with the people of Canaan resulted in turning a relatively short trip into a grueling forty-year trek.

THE SERPENT IS A DEFEATED ENEMY. The significance of a serpent being the source of death was not lost on the people of Israel. They knew it was the serpent who fomented rebellion in the Garden of Eden. They also understood the significance of Moses' response. It was not unusual for an ancient army to rally around the head of a defeated general impaled on a stake. Impaling a bronze serpent on a stake and holding it high was a proclamation that the enemy had been defeated.

GOD VALUES SIMPLE OBEDIENCE OVER RELIGIOUS RITUAL. Those bitten by the snakes did not have to go through complicated healing ceremonies or develop a vaccine. The real poison was not snake venom but rebellion against God's chosen leader. The cure was deceptively simple. The only thing commanded was that the dying people literally "look up" to Moses again as God's chosen leader.

1446 BC Aaron builds an idol of a golden calf

c. 3500 BC Wadjet, a snake goddess worshiped as one of the early Egyptian deities

c.1600 BC Minoans worship a snake goddess on Crete

Because they refused to trust God and enter Canaan, the Israelites had to wander in the desert for forty years. At one point of this trek, God responded to his treasonous people by sending a plague of venomous snakes. God directed Moses to fashion a snake from bronze and impale it on a pole. All who looked at this snake were healed from the effects of the serpents' venom.

DAILY READING PLAN
March 16: Exodus 32
March 17: Numbers 13, 14
March 18: Numbers 21:4-9

When it happened...
1446–1406 BC

Where it happened...
In the desert

ITS PART IN GOD'S PLAN

Because of their disobedience, every Israelite over twenty years of age (with the exception of Joshua and Caleb) would die during the forty years of desert wandering. An entirely different generation would enter the promised land. And one who had remained faithful despite opposition would lead them.

1445 BC Only Joshua and Caleb recommend attacking Canaan

Sometime between 1445–1406 BC Moses constructs a bronze serpent

c. 1200 BC Rod of Asclepius, a snake coiled around a staff, becomes a symbol for the practice of medicine

Shortly after the people of Israel left Egypt, the sight of that entire nation on the move stirred resistance in the people living in the lands through which they passed. When the Amalekites attacked, Moses commissioned Joshua the son of Nun to lead the Israelite army into battle. When spies were chosen to reconnoiter Canaan, Joshua and

JOSHUA, MOSES'

When it happened...
1406 BC

Where it happened...
East of the Jordan River near Mt. Nebo

DAILY READING PLAN
March 19: Exodus 17:8-16
March 20: Exodus 33:7-11
March 21: Deuteronomy 34

ITS PART IN GOD'S PLAN

The wait was over. God would fulfill his promise to Abram and deliver a land that he had vowed to give his descendants. Leading the people out into their new life was Joshua, a man whose very name meant "Jehovah/Yahweh saves." Centuries later God would command that a newborn baby be given the same name. We know this Savior by the Greek rather than the Hebrew pronunciation of his name—Jesus.

1446 BC Joshua leads battle against the Amalekites

1445 BC Joshua and Caleb reconnoiter Canaan

Caleb were the only two of the twelve who were willing to enter the promised land. Joshua continued to serve as Moses' aide as Moses brought God's words to the people.

God did not permit Moses to enter Canaan, but allowed him to view it from the summit of Mount Nebo. After Moses' death Joshua took leadership of the people of Israel.

SUCCESSOR

MAJOR THEMES

GODLY LEADERS ARE CALLED TO PREPARE OTHERS TO TAKE RESPONSIBILITY. No one can do it alone. No one can do it forever. Though Moses displayed a remarkable youthfulness as he led the people through the wilderness, he was 120 years old at the end of the journey. But from the beginning Moses had nurtured a successor who would have the faith and courage to handle the challenges ahead.

EVEN THE BEST AMONG US HARBOR REBELLION AGAINST GOD. Adam and Eve wanted to be like God. Apparently even someone like Moses was not immune from that temptation. God commanded Moses to speak to a rock in the desert of Zin, and God would provide water for the thirsty and complaining people. Instead, Moses stood with Aaron, struck the rock, and seems to have taken credit for the miracle himself. For that reason, God told Moses that he would not lead the people into Canaan. In the end, it was not Moses' age or health that kept him out of the promised land. It was this display of rebellion and arrogance.

COURAGE IS THE RESULT OF FAITH. We could not imagine a baseball manager letting a starting pitcher make his debut in the deciding World Series game. It would be unthinkable to have a novice physician attempt a complicated heart bypass as his first surgery. Yet God placed newly commissioned (though not inexperienced) Joshua in charge and sent him before the people as they entered Canaan. When Joshua had encouraged the people to enter Canaan four decades earlier, he stood opposed to nearly all of Israel. He did so because he trusted that the victory would come from the God who entered the land in front of them.

1406 BC Joshua becomes Moses' successor

c. 1350 BC War chariot introduced in China

c. 1000 BC Battering rams used in Assyria (modern Iran)

As they did four decades earlier, the nation of Israel stood poised to enter Canaan. But unlike the previous occasion, a whole new generation stood willing to trust God to keep his promise. Led by the hand of God, the Israelites conquered city after city until most of the land was under their control.

JUDGMENT OF

DAILY READING PLAN

When it happened...
1406–1385 BC

March 22: Joshua 1
March 23: Joshua 2

Where it happened...
Canaan

March 24: Joshua 6
March 25: Joshua 23

MAJOR THEMES

SOME LESSONS BEAR REPEATING. The generation entering the promised land had missed some key lessons. They were not of age when the first Passover was celebrated, the sea was crossed, or when the first spies made their report. So God held a review session. Two (not twelve this time) spies were sent out, the Jordan was crossed on dry ground, and another Passover was celebrated.

JUDGMENT IS AN UGLY NECESSITY. The idea of complete annihilation at the command of God seems barbaric to the modern mind. The Bible does not hide this event, but three things should be considered. First, the Canaanite society was so corrupt that it practiced infant sacrifice and forced its young men and women into both homosexual and heterosexual prostitution as a religious duty. Second, God's motivation was not primarily one of wrath but of love—he did not want the Israelites to be victims of such a decadent society. Finally, the opportunity to avoid judgment by simple, obedient faith was afforded to one of the least in that society—a prostitute named Rahab and her family. Judgment, though unspeakably ugly, is always paired with love and salvation when it comes from God.

EACH GENERATION FACES A TIME OF DECISION. Just as Joshua was called on to serve his generation in the name of God, he called on the next generation to do the same. Nearing the end of his life, Joshua challenged Israel to remember who they were and to renew the covenant with the one who brought them where they were.

1406 BC Israel enters Canaan and conquers Jericho

1504–1492 BC Egypt conquers parts of the Arabian Peninsula

The giving of manna stopped as soon as they entered Canaan, never to appear again. Joshua continued to lead as God's appointed judge, or deputy, into his old age. But the true king of Israel was not a man.

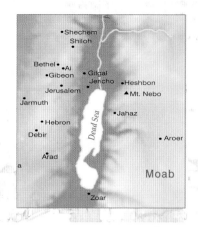

CANAAN

ITS PART IN GOD'S PLAN

God kept the promises he had made to Abraham centuries earlier. Thousands of Abraham's descendants settled into the land God had promised them. God had gone with them from Egypt, leading them as their king. But would this nation fulfill its purpose of being a blessing to the world by showing what it is like to be ruled by God alone?

1406–1385 BC Conquest of Canaan by Israel

1385 BC Joshua's farewell address and plea for faithfulness

c. 1310 BC Hindu holy book, the Bhagavad Gita, is written

There was never a nation like Israel, nor has there been one since. Israel was a nation founded by God, structured by God, and ruled by God. As the people settled into Canaan, the nation was an alliance of tribes united under God alone. As long as they were loyal to God, their only king, they were victorious and expelled the pagan inhabitants of Canaan.

RULE BY
THE JUDGES

When it happened...
1385–1050 BC

Where it happened...
Canaan

OUT OF SIGHT, OUT OF MIND. Like Adam and Eve in the Garden of Eden, humans foolishly continue to believe they can hide from an omnipresent God. When the visible leadership of a judge of Israel was gone, the people acted as if God were no longer king. Instead of obeying the Law of Moses, they lived by situation ethics that led to the ugliest moral failings.

GOD IS IN CHARGE, NOT MEN OR WOMEN. While ancient societies were almost always male dominated, Israel was designed as a theocracy in which both men and women lived to their fullest. When selecting a judge to free Israel from King Jabin of Canaan, Deborah was God's choice. She deputized Barak, but another woman struck the ultimate blow of the resistance. Jael, armed only with a hammer and a tent peg, put an end to Jabin's ruthless general, Sisera.

MIGHTY WARRIORS IN GOD'S ARMY MAY NOT NEED WEAPONS! To free Israel from the Midianites, God chose a rather insignificant man who was concealing his crops from the invaders. God addressed Gideon as a "mighty warrior" despite his limitations—and had Gideon gather an army. But then God commanded that he reduce his forces to a bare minimum. Finally, armed with torches and trumpets (and the presence of God!), the army routed the oppressors.

1385 BC
Death of Joshua

1334–1325 BC
King Tut in Egypt

But that was not to last. The Israelites allowed some inhabitants to stay, and even began to mix pagan religions with the commands of God. When this happened, they fell prey to attacking armies and even civil strife. Finally, when life reached a low point, the people called to God. He responded by appointing a judge—a deputy under direct divine command—to restore peace. Yet soon after peace was restored, the cycle was repeated. Among those judges were familiar names such as Deborah, Gideon, and Samson. But whenever a visible human leader was gone, the country inevitably sank into moral chaos.

DAILY READING PLAN

March 26: Judges 2:6-23; 21:25
March 27: Judges 4
March 28: Judges 6, 7
March 29: Judges 13–16

ITS PART IN GOD'S PLAN

The period of judges was a dark period in the history of Israel. The people continued to turn from God, but in his grace he delivered them time after time by way of some of the least likely human instruments. This period illustrated that without a human leader commanding the armies, the people did what was right in their own eyes.

1239–1199 BC
Deborah, Barak,
and the Canaanites

1192–1152 BC
Gideon and the
Midianites

1100–1080 BC
Samson and the
Philistines

c. 1193 BC Greeks destroy Troy
(the Trojan Horse legend)

Near the end of the tumultuous period of the judges, a tender love story played out. During a famine in Israel, a Jewish family relocated to Moab, probably having to sell their family land in the process. While in Moab, the sons married Moabite women. During that time the father and both sons died, leaving only Naomi and her two foreign daughters-in-law. Naomi decided to return to Israel and live out her days supported by her family. She urged Ruth and Orpah to remain in Moab to marry Moabite men, knowing that their prospects as foreign, penniless widows in

THE REDEMPTION

DAILY READING PLAN

March 30: Leviticus 19:9, 10; 23:22;
Deuteronomy 24:19-22;
25:5-10
March 31: Ruth 1
April 1: Ruth 2
April 2: Ruth 3
April 3: Ruth 4

ITS PART IN GOD'S PLAN

In Ruth we see not only the beginning of the royal line of Israel; we see a much larger plan at work. The idea of redemption in the Law of Moses will become the picture of God's relationship to humankind. God the Redeemer wants to bring the spiritually bankrupt one (all people) back into his family by making her his bride (the church).

c. 1100 BC Ruth comes to Bethlehem with Naomi, gathers grain in the fields of Boaz

c. 1100 BC Ruth marries Boaz

HAJOR

From c. 1200 BC Olmec civilization in what is now south-central Mexico. Olmecs practiced slash-and-burn agriculture, clearing forests to replace over-cultivated fields.

Israel were bleak. Ruth refused, pledging allegiance not only to Naomi but also to the God of Israel.

In Israel, Ruth supported herself and Naomi by picking unharvested grain in the field of a man named Boaz. As it happened, Boaz was an unmarried member of Naomi's family. Boaz married Ruth and restored the inheritance of Naomi by fathering descendants to her family. One of those descendants was Obed, who would become the grandfather of King David.

OF RUTH

When it happened...
c. 1100 BC

Where it happened...
Moab and Bethlehem

MAJOR THEMES

EXAMPLE IS A GREAT TEACHER. Moabites were despised, considered to be the product of an incestuous relationship between Lot and his daughter. The courage it took for Ruth to move to a land where she would be penniless and hated is remarkable. But the courage may have been born of a faith she saw in her mother-in-law (however imperfect).

THE LAW OF MOSES PROVIDED FOR THE POWERLESS. The account of Ruth seems strange to those unfamiliar with Jewish Law. The poor could support themselves because of the law of gleaning. Landowners were forbidden from thoroughly harvesting their crops, allowing the poor to live on that which was left. Furthermore, the Law allowed for a widow to be restored to her husband's family and inheritance by marrying his closest available male relative.

GOD'S KINGDOM IS THE LEAST EXCLUSIVE PLACE ON EARTH. Even though she was from the most humble of origins, Ruth was allotted a place in the line of Abraham. Not only that, she became the ancestor of King David of Israel . . . and an even greater king born centuries later in Bethlehem.

c. 700 BC Chinese begin water conservation projects and irrigation

c. 500 BC First evidence of tea drinking in India

While serving as a priest/judge at the tabernacle, Eli saw a woman in great distress as she prayed. Eli asked the Lord to grant her request. The childless Hannah's plea for a son was granted, and she dedicated that son, Samuel, to the service of God at the tabernacle. Samuel was reared by Eli and succeeded Eli as judge.

During that time the Philistines from the west were at war with Israel. At one point they captured the ark of the covenant and placed their trophy in the temple

SAMUEL, THE

When it happened...
1105–c. 1018 BC

Where it happened...
Shiloh

DAILY READING PLAN

April 4: 1 Samuel 1, 2
April 5: 1 Samuel 3, 4
April 6: 1 Samuel 5, 6
April 7: 1 Samuel 7

1105 BC Samuel is dedicated to God's service at Shiloh

1105–1080 BC Samuel serves at Shiloh with Eli

of their god Dagon. Yet, as happened in Egypt at the time of Moses, God met this challenge to his omnipotence with plagues, until the ark was returned along with tribute. Under the leadership of Samuel, the Philistine threat was quelled for a time at the town of Mizpah. Outside Mizpah, Samuel put up a memorial stone commemorating God's intervention in securing the victory. He called it by a name familiar to us: Ebenezer, meaning "stone of help."

LAST JUDGE

ITS PART IN GOD'S PLAN

The time of the judges was coming to an end. Israel continued its cycle of rebellion, repentance, and restoration, only to rebel once again. Samuel would usher in a new era of leadership to this nation of loosely associated tribes.

MAJOR THEMES

GOD HEARS. The name Samuel means "heard of God." Hannah prayed and God heard. God spoke and Samuel, even as a child, heard. Samuel spoke the words of God, and the people of Israel recognized that God heard them and communicated with them.

GOD HAS NO GRANDCHILDREN. A relationship with God is not inherited. Eli was a godly judge, but his sons Hophni and Phinehas used their service at God's tabernacle for personal gain. Like Aaron's sons, who dared treat serving as a liaison between God and humankind capriciously, Eli's sons paid the price of traitors.

THERE IS ONE GOD. The account of the ark of the covenant in the temple of Dagon is humorous. The Philistines returned after placing the ark in the temple, only to find their idol prostrate, "bowing" before the ark! After righting the statue, they returned later to find the idol prostrate once more with both head and hands broken off. False gods have no ability to act or think, but God is present on earth!

1080 BC Philistines capture the ark of the covenant and place it in the temple of Dagon

1060 BC Led by Samuel, Israelites defeat the Philistines at Mizpah

Philistine gods:

 Baal

 ZAGARBAL

 Astarte

 Dagon

When Samuel grew old, he set his sons up as the next judges, but as was the case with Eli, Samuel's sons used their authority for personal gain. Frustrated with the system of judges, the leaders of Israel came to Samuel and demanded that Israel become a military monarchy, similar to the surrounding nations. Samuel, angered, brought that demand to God. Even though the people were rejecting God as their king, God relented but told Samuel to warn them of the consequences of human leadership.

Saul of the tribe of Benjamin appeared to be an excellent choice for a monarch and commander in chief. A physically imposing warrior, Saul stood a full head taller

SAUL AND THE

ITS PART IN GOD'S PLAN

Under Saul, Israel was changed from a tribal coalition into a monarchy. Military authority was no longer given on an ad hoc basis, as it had been with the judges, but was consolidated in the office of king. Although Israel rejected God by asking for a human king, it would be through a royal lineage that God would establish his eternal kingdom.

DAILY READING PLAN

April 8: 1 Samuel 8
April 9: 1 Samuel 9:1–10:1
April 10: 1 Samuel 13:1-15
April 11: 1 Samuel 15

When it happened...
1050–1010 BC

Where it happened...
Areas in the land allotted to the tribe of Benjamin

1050 BC Elders of Israel demand a king, Samuel anoints Saul as king

1050 BC Saul offers an unauthorized sacrifice after a battle with the Philistines

1100 BC Phoenician traders begin spreading the alphabet throughout the Mediterranean area

than the average Israelite. At God's command, Samuel anointed (poured oil on, as a symbol of being covered by God's Spirit) Saul as king. But soon Saul began to assume authority that was not his. After a battle with the Philistines, he assumed a priestly role and offered an unauthorized sacrifice. Later, in a battle with the Amalekites, Saul blatantly spurned the rules of engagement ordered by Samuel. Instead of operating as a civil authority under God, Saul thought his position empowered him to make his own rules. Though Saul would remain on the throne for almost two more decades, God had rejected him as king.

OFFICE OF KING

MAJOR THEMES

IF ALL ELSE FAILS, BLAME GOD! The problem with rule by God-appointed deputies was not with the system but with the people. By refusing to show allegiance to God as king of Israel, the nation suffered at the hands of their enemies. But unwilling to take the blame for not leading their people to follow the commands of God, the elders of Israel blamed God for being an inadequate military leader! They demanded to have a visible king lead them into battle, rather than be loyal to the God who would protect them from their enemies.

POWER CORRUPTS HUMAN LEADERS. The rebellious attitude of human-kind can be magnified when authority is granted to a human leader. Aaron's sons, Eli's sons, and Samuel's sons were quick to try to expand the limited power granted them. When the governance of the nation and the command of the army were granted to Saul, he had the power of life and death over his subjects. He became a victim of his own success and forgot that he was called to *follow* the rules, not *make* them.

GOD LIMITS THE AUTHORITY OF HUMAN LEADERS. Saul refused to be the kind of king he was called to be, so his power would end. God did not physically remove him from the throne until God's replacement was ready, but the authority given Saul was rescinded.

1025 BC God rejects Saul as king after battle with the Amalekites

1010 BC
Death of King Saul

c. 1000–900 BC
Phoenicians colonize Spain with settlement at Cadiz

Though Saul would remain on the throne another fifteen years, God ordered Samuel to go to the house of Jesse (grandson of Ruth and Boaz) and anoint a new king whom God would choose. Jesse's older sons had the appearance one would expect in a warrior king, but God rejected them. He ordered Samuel to christen Jesse's youngest son, David, as Israel's king. While everyone would expect a king to be a warrior, God chose a shepherd to be a king.

David's fame grew, ironically, because of the skills he had honed as a shepherd. As Saul continued to grasp power without fully embracing the direction of God, he became

DAVID, THE SHEPHERD KING

MAJOR THEMES

INTERNAL CHARACTER TRUMPS EXTERNAL APPEARANCE. God told a shocked Samuel that he saw in David the makings of a king that were invisible to the human eye. While Saul was a head taller than his peers, David was the runt of the family compared to his brothers. But David shared a shepherd's mind-set with God, something that was not true of the others.

FIGHTING GOD'S LEADING IS A LOSING PROPOSITION. When Saul rejected the leadership of God, his mental state started to collapse. The power and security of following God was gone, and in their place were fear, bitterness, and envy. As was the case when Adam and Eve tried to do life their way, the world Saul found himself in was a much more hostile place.

GOD USES THE SKILLS AND PASSIONS WE HAVE. When David put on Saul's armor to fight Goliath, it was obvious he was trying to be something he was not. Unlike Goliath, who was born and bred for battle, David was a shepherd who wrote songs, played the harp, and had the courage to face wild animals with only a rock and a sling. God called David to use the skills and passions he had been given and be the king God wanted him to be.

1025 BC
Samuel anoints
David as king

ALENSHA

c. 1150 BC Aristocrats in
Egypt begin using chairs

increasingly unstable. David first entered the court of Saul to soothe Saul with his harp playing, a skill he had developed while he was minding sheep.

When Goliath the Philistine challenged any soldier of Israel to a duel, he found no takers among the warrior class. Instead, David confronted the giant from Gath with the offensive weapon he used to protect his flock. With a sling, a stone, and Goliath's own sword, David ended the threat. As a result, David found favor among the populace—but engendered jealousy in the mind of the king.

When it happened...
1025 BC

Where it happened...
The Valley of Elah

DAILY READING PLAN

April 12: 1 Samuel 16:1-13

April 13: 1 Samuel 16:14-23;
Psalm 23

April 14: 1 Samuel 17

ITS PART IN GOD'S PLAN

When Jacob prophesied concerning his sons centuries before, he predicted that the line of Judah would rule Israel. Saul, of the line of Benjamin, rejected God's commands, and David stepped in and fulfilled the ancient vision.

1025 BC
David serves in
Saul's court

1025 BC
David faces Goliath

c. 1000 BC Latins migrate
to Italy from the Danube
Valley region

David, the Shepherd King · 71

Saul's jealousy of David increased in proportion to David's popularity. Saul's attempts on David's life were as overt as hurling a spear at him and as subversive as sending him into battle with the Philistines in order to pay for his daughter's hand in marriage. Soon David had to flee for his life.

For fifteen years, David built and led a band of soldiers who eluded Saul's

DAVID AND

ITS PART IN GOD'S PLAN

God is patient. He does not act capriciously. Although Saul had arrogantly used his role as king for self-aggrandizement, God allowed him to remain on the throne for fifteen more years. But Saul did not use those years to change his course and allow God to rule through him. Instead, he attempted to use force to hold on to his power and eliminate opposition that God had placed there. As a result, Saul's life continued to spiral out of control, ending in his death.

MAJOR THEMES

LOYALTY TO GOD MUST SUPERSEDE ALL OTHER RELATIONSHIPS. It was obvious to many that God was with David. Although Jonathan, the son of Saul, was heir apparent, he protected David rather than allow his father to kill the man that would take his place on the throne. Michal, daughter of Saul, refused to be a pawn of her father and use her marriage to David to neutralize his threat to the throne. She protected him though it distanced her from her own father.

RESPECT THE POSITION EVEN WHEN THE PERSON HOLDING IT IS UNWORTHY. David understood what Saul did not. God was the king of Israel, even though a human being sat on the throne. Despite the fact that Saul had tried to kill David, he still held the position granted him by God. Imperfect people still hold positions of power in this world. The authority granted by God must be respected even when a scoundrel temporarily wields it.

LET GOD BE GOD. Abram and Sarai had tried centuries earlier to fulfill God's promise through their own efforts. David refused to make that mistake. Though he was promised the throne, David refused to use assassination to place himself there.

1025 BC Saul's daughter Michal and son Jonathan side with David over Saul

c. 1045 BC Beginning of the Zhou Dynasty in China. Developed the idea that a ruler was in power by the "mandate of Heaven."

army while also repelling foreign incursions into the land of Israel. On two occasions God delivered a helpless Saul into the hands of David and his men. Although David's soldiers encouraged him to kill Saul and take the throne by force, David refused. David did not assume the throne until Saul was mortally wounded in battle against the Philistines.

SAUL

When it happened...
1025–1010 BC

Where it happened...
Israel and the land of the Philistines

DAILY READING PLAN

April 15: 1 Samuel 19:11-16; 20:5-7, 24-42
April 16: 1 Samuel 24, 26
April 17: 1 Samuel 31

1025–1010 BC
Saul pursues David, and on two occasions David spares his life

1010 BC
Death of Saul

JOHN CAMPANA

993 BC Amenemope succeeds Psusennes I as king of Egypt

The death of Saul left a power vacuum in Israel. David became king in Judah, while Saul's son Ish-Bosheth claimed the throne in the northern regions of Israel. Within seven years, David and his armies conquered the opposition and united all Israel under his leadership. David and his armies took the city of Jerusalem from

DAVID'S REIGN

When it happened...
1010–970 BC

Where it happened...
Jerusalem and all of Israel

DAILY READING PLAN
April 18: 2 Samuel 5:1-10; 6
April 19: 2 Samuel 7
April 20: 2 Samuel 9

1010 BC Death of Saul; David assumes throne in Judah

c. 1089 BC Death of Melanthus, legendary king of Athens

the Jebusites and made it the capital of the nation. David quickly acted in ways that distinguished him from his predecessor. Upon establishing Jerusalem as his capital city, David had the ark of the covenant brought there—an act recognizing God as the true king of Israel. Furthermore, David desired to build a temple as a permanent residence for the ark. God delayed those plans however.

In another departure from the norm, David sought out a remaining descendant of Saul. He found Mephibosheth, not to eliminate him as a threat but to show kindness to him in honor of Saul's son (and David's ally) Jonathan. Though Mephibosheth was disabled and could not work to support himself, David brought him into the palace to live.

ITS PART IN GOD'S PLAN

David modeled the humility that Saul lacked. In recognizing that the office of king was only a temporary manifestation of the eternal sovereignty of God, David set the standard of a godly monarch against which all succeeding kings of Israel would be measured.

<table>
<tr><td rowspan="3">MAJOR THEMES</td><td>

BE A PART OF GOD'S PLAN; DON'T JUST INVITE HIM TO BE PART OF YOURS. David's motives were good. He saw himself living in a palace while the ark of the covenant, the presence of the true king of Israel, remained in a tent. It made sense to "do God a favor" by building a temple. But before acting, David asked. And he changed his plans to conform to God's will.

CELEBRATE IN GOD'S PRESENCE. Common wisdom dictates that royals behave with a sense of decorum. But knowing the importance of bringing the ark of the covenant into Jerusalem, David celebrated the occasion with exuberant joy. His wife Michal, daughter of Saul, criticized him for his casual dress and unrestrained festivity. David responded that lowering himself before the presence of God was not vulgarity, but propriety of the highest level.

VALUE PEOPLE OVER SELF-PRESERVATION. Jonathan had alienated himself from his father Saul and even put his own life in danger for David. Though in direct line for the throne, Jonathan knew that it belonged to David, not him. Fittingly, David brought the son of Jonathan into the palace to honor his memory.

</td></tr>
</table>

1003 BC David becomes king of all Israel

1003 BC David conquers Jerusalem and brings the ark of the covenant to Jerusalem

967 BC Tiglath-Pileser II becomes king of Assyria

NATHAN AND THE OFFICE OF PROPHET

DAILY READING PLAN

April 21: 2 Samuel 11
April 22: 2 Samuel 12; Psalm 51
April 23: 2 Samuel 13
April 24: 2 Samuel 18

When it happened...
997 BC

Where it happened...
Jerusalem

ITS PART IN GOD'S PLAN

Prophets would play a key role in the history of the kingdom of Israel. They would boldly confront abuse of power, but would also point to the future when God would send one who would be prophet, priest, and king.

997 BC
Nathan confronts David
over Bathsheba

c. 997–980 BC
Absalom's insurrection
grows and is defeated

c. 970 BC
Death of David

David's power grew, and threats from without were being neutralized. But threats from within had just begun. David, who may have had seven wives at the time, took his next wife from another man. To make matters worse, he used the power of his army to take the life of that man.

While God had used prophets (also called seers) to bring his message to his people, the monarchy gave the office of prophet even greater importance. It was necessary to rein in the civil authority of a king who abused his power. Nathan was such a prophet, and he did just that. Nathan boldly confronted David about his adultery and murder and pronounced God's judgment on him and his family.

There were problems with children of multiple wives all living within the palace—problems that led to sordid tales of rape, murder, and sedition. Absalom, David's son by his wife Maacah, led a revolution that nearly destroyed David's kingdom.

MAJOR THEMES

WE CAN BE SPOILED BY SUCCESS. David's early military successes may have led to complacency. For his spring military campaign, David sent his general Joab off to war, but stayed behind. During that time a sleepless David saw Bathsheba, wife of one of his soldiers, bathing. Aroused by the unclad beautiful woman and having the political power to do as he wished, David took a course that ended with a murder to cover up the pregnancy of another man's wife.

HUMAN AUTHORITY IS GRANTED, YET CHECKED, BY GOD. Modern ideas concerning separation of political powers were not the norm in the ancient world. The king often held political power, military power, and religious authority. In Israel that was not the case. Priests were the only authorized agents for interceding with God for the wrongdoing of the people. The king commanded the military but could not offer sacrifices or lead other religious events. Finally, God could at any time communicate with a prophet separate from the throne and the priesthood in order to restrain the power of either.

LEADING A FAMILY IS A CRUCIAL RESPONSIBILITY. David, like other monarchs throughout the centuries, took wives as spoils of war and used marriage as a way to secure peace with other nations. This led to children by multiple wives being reared under one roof. When Amnon (son of David and Ahinoam) raped his stepsister (Tamar, daughter of David and Maacah), David was angry but took no decisive action. As a result, Tamar's brother Absalom took matters into his own hands, killing Amnon and nearly removing David from the throne.

History is filled with stories of intrigue inside palace walls:

Greek playwright Sophocles (c. 497–405 BC) told the story of Oedipus the king. Oedipus was the abandoned son of Laius, king of Thebes. After killing the king and taking Laius's wife as his own, it was discovered that Oedipus had married his own mother.

Roman emperor Caligula was assassinated by members of his own guard in AD 41 and replaced by his uncle Claudius.

King Faisal of Saudi Arabia was murdered by his nephew Faisal bin Musa'id in AD 1975.

During the latter days of David's reign, David made plans for his (and Bathsheba's) son Solomon to succeed him. Together they planned for the construction of the temple on a site chosen by God. The temple would be built at the very place Abraham had been commanded to sacrifice Isaac centuries earlier.

SOLOMON AND THE TEMPLE

When it happened...
970–930 BC

Where it happened...
Jerusalem

GOD PAINTS HIS STORY ON THE CANVAS OF HUMAN HISTORY AND GEOGRAPHY. "Location, location, location" is more than a contemporary slogan about real estate. The site for the temple was not a place arbitrarily chosen by David or Solomon. The temple would be the site of ceremonial sacrifice. So God wanted it placed where he had shown Abraham that he would provide a substitute payment for that which Abraham truly owed God. God orchestrated history in order to teach a lesson the whole world would eventually be told—the only way humankind can settle the debt owed to God is for God to make arrangements to pay it himself.

GOD GIVES US MORE THAN WE ASK, WHEN WE ASK FOR THE RIGHT THINGS. Solomon's plea for wisdom was the seminal moment of his reign. Wisdom is more than knowledge. It is knowledge used with God's moral direction. Only when we invite God to direct the use of what we know are we able to obtain the abundance of what God has for us.

GODLY LEADERSHIP BENEFITS EVERYONE. The incredible wealth of Solomon could be just another story of a powerful ruler living an extravagant lifestyle. However, Solomon's wealth was gained for his subjects. The reign of Solomon was described as a time of national peace and property ownership, with each citizen living in safety under his own vine and fig tree.

980–970 BC David and Solomon make plans for the temple

970 BC Solomon assumes the throne and asks God for wisdom to rule

966–959 BC Temple construction

c. 2584–2561 BC Construction of the Great Pyramid of Giza, the largest of the Egyptian pyramids

After David's death and a period of political infighting, Solomon took the throne. Awed by the task of ruling Israel, Solomon asked God not for wealth or fame but for wisdom to discharge the duties of the throne in a godly manner. God granted this request, along with a promise of wealth and fame.

Construction began in the fourth year of Solomon's reign and continued for seven years. When the temple was dedicated, fire descended from Heaven to consume sacrifices offered there, and God made his presence known to all observers.

ITS PART IN GOD'S PLAN

While the wisdom and wealth of Solomon were more than impressive, the real accomplishment of his reign was the construction of the temple. The center of sacrifice and religious festivals, the temple was the hub of the nation and the symbol of national identity.

DAILY READING PLAN

April 25: 1 Chronicles 22
April 26: 1 Kings 3:1-15; 4:20-28
April 27: 1 Kings 6
April 28: 2 Chronicles 5–7

959 BC
Dedication of
the temple

959–930 BC
Israel enjoys great
prosperity

c. 605–562 BC Construction of
the Hanging Gardens of Babylon,
75-foot-high multilevel gardens
with machinery for watering

c. 280 BC The Lighthouse
of Alexandria, one of the
tallest structures on earth
for centuries

The allure of power took another victim. Solomon built a harem of one thousand women as a "perk" of his throne. Seven hundred were from royal families. That seems to indicate that the purpose for many of his unions was political expediency. But instead of bringing peace to Israel, Solomon's wives led him to abandon the only one who could bring peace.

SOLOMON'S

When it happened...
Sometime between
959–930 BC

Where it happened...
On a road out of Jerusalem

970–930 BC Solomon marries
700 women of royal birth
and has 300 concubines

Sometime between 959–930 BC
Ahijah, a prophet, tells Jeroboam
that he will be successful in
leading the 10 northern tribes to
independence from the rest of Israel

c. 1070 BC Kingdom
of Cush established
on the Blue Nile

Hadad the Edomite and Rezon, son of the king of Zobah, harassed the kingdom from without. Jeroboam, whom Solomon had appointed labor secretary of the northern tribes, used his position to undermine the king. Ahijah the prophet predicted a civil war that would occur after Solomon's death.

DOWNFALL

ITS PART IN GOD'S PLAN

The reigns of David and Solomon comprised the golden age of Israel. As great as those kings were, human weakness would bring an end to that age. But if the kingdom were divided, what would happen to the worship of God in Jerusalem?

DAILY READING PLAN
April 29: 1 Kings 11:1-13
April 30: 1 Kings 11:14-43

MAJOR THEMES

UNWISE RELATIONSHIPS CAN CAUSE US TO COMPROMISE OUR KEY VALUES. The intimacy shared between husband and wife is a gift of God. Part of the value of that intimacy is that a godly spouse can influence the other in a positive way. Unfortunately, the opposite is also true. A spouse who rejects God can lead the other to reject him.

LIFE DOES NOT WORK WELL WITHOUT THE AUTHOR OF IT. While it may have made sense to Solomon to create alliances through marriage, it just did not work. At the end of his reign, Solomon's kingdom was threatened by kingdoms he probably thought he'd appeased by taking a wife from the respective royal families and adopting some of their religious practices. Furthermore, a man whom Solomon had promoted into leadership began a subversive campaign within the government itself.

A MIGHTY POLITICAL FORCE CAN BE TOTALLY DESTROYED WITHIN ONE GENERATION. The prophets often offered truth with a memorable performance. Ahijah illustrated a coming split between the twelve tribes of Israel by ripping a new cloak into twelve pieces. Just as his cloak was a new piece of apparel one moment and scrap the next, an entire nation can be reduced to warring factions if not united by the commands of God.

930 BC
Death of Solomon

c. 900 BC Yajnavalkya describes the motions of the sun and moon in the ancient Indian work Satapatha Brahmana

Rehoboam assumed the throne and was petitioned by the labor force to ease their workload. After consulting both his elders and his peers, Rehoboam followed the advice of his peers to take a hard line against the request. As a result, Jeroboam, who had

REHOBOAM AND

DAILY READING PLAN
May 1: 1 Kings 12:1-24; 14:21-31
May 2: 1 Kings 15:1-5;
2 Kings 8:16-19, 25-27;
2 Chronicles 28:1-4; 33:1-9
May 3: 1 Kings 15:9-15

ITS PART IN GOD'S PLAN

Civil war could not destroy the nation God created. For the centuries following Rehoboam, Judah had its ups and downs. And God used those times to again illustrate that allowing God to rule through an obedient human king kept him from having to rule *despite* a human king.

930 BC Rehoboam's stubbornness leads to the secession of the 10 northern tribes

930–586 BC Kings of Judah rule

c. 850–750 BC Homer's *Iliad* and *Odyssey* written

supervised the work force for Solomon, was able to lead the ten northern tribes in seceding from the rest of the nation. Jeroboam became the king of this northern kingdom (called Israel or Samaria), leaving Rehoboam to rule the southern kingdom (called Judah).

THE SOUTHERN KINGDOM

When it happened...
930 BC

Where it happened...
Judah

MAJOR THEMES

BAD ADVICE IS FREE AND WORTH EVERY PENNY. The advice offered by the elders of Israel was based on their experience under the rule of Solomon. The nation was prosperous and at peace and could afford to ease production and enjoy the fruits of the nation's golden age. Yet Rehoboam's peers could not see beyond their limited experiences. To them, compassion was a sign of weakness; acquiescence could lead Rehoboam to lose control. Unfortunately, just the opposite was true.

GODLY LEADERS PROVIDE A BENCHMARK FOR EVALUATING OUR OWN SUCCESS. Rehoboam (and the kings who ruled after him) had the choice of following the example of the autocrat Saul or the shepherd David. Rehoboam took the road of Saul, caring more about self-preservation and personal security than the needs of those under his care. Kings who looked out for themselves were likely to compromise the religious and social commands of the Law of God. This inevitably resulted in pagan worship and shedding of innocent blood.

LESS CAN BE MORE WHEN GOD IS IN IT. Common sense tells us that the king who took ten tribes with him had more than the king who was left with the remaining two tribes. And common sense would be wrong. Judah had the temple of God in Jerusalem. No number of human beings can be an adequate substitute for the presence and power of God.

586 BC
Judah conquered
by Babylon

772 BC Construction begins on the Temple of Artemis at Ephesus, one of the Seven Wonders of the Ancient World

During the brief power vacuum after the death of Solomon, Jeroboam gathered with the Israelites to confront the new king, Rehoboam, about reducing their labor. When the request was not granted, Jeroboam led the revolt that split the kingdom. But the people of Israel were required to go to the temple in Jerusalem to observe

JEROBOAM AND

When it happened...
930 BC

Where it happened...
Israel

DAILY READING PLAN
May 4: 1 Kings 12:25-33
May 5: 1 Kings 14:1-20
May 6: 2 Kings 17

MAJOR THEMES

REPEATED MISTAKES BRING REPEATED RESULTS. Years earlier in the wilderness, Aaron presented a golden calf to the Israelites instead of insisting that they trust the God who had just given them the Law from Sinai. Jeroboam offered two golden calves instead of insisting that his people worship in the temple in Jerusalem. This lack of trust angered God in both cases.

GOD IS PATIENT. It may seem remarkable that a nation that flagrantly rejected God would be allowed to exist for two more centuries. But it does illustrate that God is not just waiting for people to make one misstep so that he can condemn them. God continued to offer the northern kingdom the opportunity to turn back to him. Yet not one king took him up on his offer of forgiveness and restoration.

A NATION CAN BE RELIGIOUS WITHOUT BEING GODLY. The northern kingdom was nothing if not religious. Unlike the southern kingdom, it had two, not just one, national places of worship. Like the southern kingdom, they offered sacrifices, supported a priesthood, and held religious festivals. But without obedience to God, their religious practices were meaningless.

930 BC Jeroboam establishes an alternative religious system in the northern kingdom

930–722 BC Kings of Israel reign in the northern kingdom

major religious festivals. Because Jeroboam feared that religious unity would lead to political unity, he set up his own ungodly religious system in the north. As always, the desire to have power apart from God led only to destruction. Two centuries after Jeroboam's rebellion, Assyria conquered the northern kingdom.

THE NORTHERN KINGDOM

ITS PART IN GOD'S PLAN

In many ways, the northern kingdom served as an example to the southern kingdom of what *not* to do! The rebellion and compromise of their relatives in the north should have convinced the south to stay true to the commands of God and the example set by David and his rule. But that was not to be.

722 BC Assyria conquers the northern kingdom

883 BC Revival of Assyrian power under Ashurnasirpal II

671 BC Assyria conquers Egypt

Less than six decades after Jeroboam tried to reinvent the worship of the God of Abraham, King Ahab embraced full-blown paganism. His wife, Jezebel, from a nation north of Israel, brought the worship of Baal with her. God responded to corruption with correction. The prophet Elijah (whose name means "God is Jehovah") confronted Ahab

ELIJAH AND ELISHA IN ISRAEL

When it happened...
870–797 BC

Where it happened...
Israel

MAJOR THEMES

WE ARE NOT ALONE. When civil authority becomes corrupt, it is easy for the people of God to feel isolated and powerless. When Elijah was at the point of giving up, God assured him that many others remained loyal to the true king of Israel. When an attacking army surrounded Elisha and his servant, God allowed them to catch a glimpse of powers greater than the armies of kings.

EVEN WHEN LEADERS ARE CORRUPT, GOD DOES NOT STOP HIS RESCUE EFFORTS. In a nation led astray by a deceitful king and queen, Elijah performed miracles that demonstrated God's power and judgment, much as Moses had done in Egypt. And just as God had given direction and nutrition and rescue to the people led by Moses, he also provided hope and sustenance to those who suffered during the rule of Ahab's family.

THE MESSAGE IS MORE IMPORTANT THAN THE MESSENGER. Although Elijah would go down in history as the example future prophets would emulate, he was not to be idolized. God actually took Elijah out of the picture before his life ended naturally. Because Elisha spoke the same message and performed powerful miracles, it was clear that the real power was not the prophet but God.

874 BC Ahab and Jezebel begin to rule Israel

870–848 BC Elijah prophesies during the reign of Ahab

895 BC Death of King Xiao of the Zhou Dynasty in China

and Jezebel and backed his message with miraculous acts. After Elijah was taken to Heaven, his protégé, Elisha ("God saves"), confronted Ahab's equally corrupt son and successor, Ahaziah. Elisha's miracles of provision and rescue complemented those of Elijah in many ways.

ITS PART IN GOD'S PLAN

Many prophets would follow Elijah, but his is the name that became synonymous with anyone called to display God's power to arrogant tyrants. God would, through bold leaders empowered by his Spirit, continue to plead with his people to return to him.

DAILY READING PLAN

May 7: 1 Kings 16:29-34; 18:16-40
May 8: 1 Kings 19
May 9: 2 Kings 2:1-18
May 10: 2 Kings 4

848 BC Elijah ascends to Heaven in a chariot of fire as Elisha looks on

848–797 BC Elisha fully dispatches the duties of the role vacated by Elijah

814 BC Traditional date for the founding of Carthage

Through Elijah and Elisha, God called Jehu to bring judgment to Ahab's family and the overt paganism they had brought to Israel. But while Jehu and later kings eschewed paganism, they perpetuated the false religious establishment founded by Jeroboam I. During the reign of Jeroboam II, God called three prophets to plead with Israel:

OTHER PROPHETS
REPENTANCE IN

When it happened...
793–715 BC

Where it happened...
Israel and Assyria

ITS PART IN GOD'S PLAN

The northern kingdom of Israel was born out of rebellion and, from the beginning, tried to come to God on its own terms. Throughout two centuries God never ceased to call Israel back. But they would not return to him.

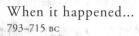

793–785 BC Jonah preaches to Nineveh in Assyria and prophesies in Israel

760–750 BC Amos preaches to Israel

c. 800 BC Rise of Greek city-states

Jonah, best known for running from God when called to confront the people of Nineveh; Amos, a simple farmer from Judah, who crossed the border to speak against the social injustice in Israel; and Hosea, who spoke to the nation that had rejected God's love— from firsthand experience of the pain of rejected love.

CALL FOR ISRAEL

DAILY READING PLAN

May 11: 2 Kings 14:23-27; Jonah 1
May 12: Jonah 3, 4
May 13: Amos 7
May 14: Hosea 1:1-3; 3:1-3; 11:1-11

MAJOR THEMES

GOD'S LOVE CROSSES BORDERS. While God was uniquely present in the temple in Jerusalem, he is not the God of one place. God showed that he was willing to forgive a cruel nation that would eventually conquer Israel. God showed that he could empower someone totally outside of the religious establishment of Israel, a warning that God would not tolerate the oppression of the powerless under the rule of Jeroboam II.

GOD'S LOVE BREAKS THE RULES. In one of the strangest and most heart-rending accounts in the Bible, God ordered Hosea to take an unfaithful wife and even take her back after she left him for another. The Law of Moses mandated the death penalty for adultery. The Law further forbade a man to remarry a woman he had divorced, after she married another. But God ordered Hosea to break the rules, because God broke the rules when it came to his bride, Israel. His nation was faithless, but he welcomed her to be his love again.

GOD'S LOVE SURPRISES EVEN THOSE WHO SPEAK HIS MESSAGE. The most unbelievable part of the account of Jonah is not the famous fish story. It is that God would send a prophet to promise judgment on the enemy of his nation and then spare them after they turned from their wrongdoing. God's mercy actually angered Jonah, who missed the point. If God would forgive an enemy that turns to him, he certainly would have welcomed Israel back to him.

753–715 BC
Hosea prophesies
in Israel

745 BC Tiglath-Pileser III becomes
the new king of Assyria and begins
to conquer neighboring nations

Shalmaneser V of Assyria discovered King Hoshea's duplicity in attempting to form an alliance against him with the king of Egypt. Assyria attacked Israel, deported the Israelites to the region of Gozan, and brought Assyrians in to resettle Israel. When God sent lions into that repopulated area, killing part of

FALL OF ISRAEL

When it happened...
722 BC

Where it happened...
Israel and Gozan

783 BC Assyria forces
Israel to pay tribute

c. 780 BC The first historic solar
eclipse is recorded in China

the population, the king of Assyria ordered a priest from Israel sent back in to teach the new residents how to worship the God of Abraham. Those residents adopted some practices taught by the priest but also mixed those with their own religious practices.

DAILY READING PLAN
May 15: 2 Kings 17:1-23
May 16: 2 Kings 17:24-41

ITS PART IN GOD'S PLAN

As was the case from the beginning, those who desire independence from God will eventually get it. For two hundred years Israel rejected the call of God to be the holy nation he intended. In doing so, they became no nation at all.

MAJOR THEMES

POLITICAL APPROACHES DO NOT SOLVE SPIRITUAL PROBLEMS. God had promised the Israelites in the time of Moses that he would protect them in their land as long as they kept his commands. But they repeatedly sought other solutions—trying to build military alliances through marriage, paying tribute, or integrating some foreign religious practices into their worship. These alliances could not ensure protection.

COMPROMISE WILL END IN A LOSS OF IDENTITY. To separate the nation, Jeroboam I had played on the tribal loyalties of the northern tribes and their envy of Judah. But in separating, the northern tribes rejected that which made them distinct from all other nations—loyalty to the God of Abraham. Today we speak of the "lost tribes of Israel," the northern tribes that were taken from their lands and integrated into the empire of their conquerors.

ALLEGIANCE TO GOD IS MORE IMPORTANT THAN GEOGRAPHY OR ETHNICITY. Many religions teach that gods control certain geographical areas. When the Assyrians tried to repopulate the land of Israel with people from their empire, they sought to appease the God who was surely angry that his land had been taken. But they failed to understand that they were dealing with the true God who created all nations and had a plan to call all nations to him.

722 BC Israel goes into captivity

727 BC Babylonia makes itself independent of Assyria

As was the case in Israel, God sent prophets to call Judah to be faithful to him, and these prophets spoke to some very specific social and political situations. Joel seems to have been written just after several years of leadership by kings who were influenced by Ahab and Jezebel in the northern kingdom. Isaiah and Micah prophesied during the

PROPHETS CALL IN JUDAH

When it happened...
835–589 BC

Where it happened...
Judah

MAJOR THEMES

THOSE WHO SPOKE FOR GOD UNDERSTOOD CURRENT EVENTS. The prophets did not speak in vague generalities. They did not prattle on about an esoteric spirituality and a generic morality. Instead, they spoke to the political turmoil of the moment. They critiqued the political alliances and compromises made by their leaders. They clearly revealed the will of God as it applied to the hopes and fears of the times in which they lived.

THOSE WHO SPOKE FOR GOD REVEALED FUTURE EVENTS. The prophets were not armchair quarterbacks who criticized the decisions of kings in retrospect. They spoke with God's authority, revealing the future results of present actions. Some contemporaries also claimed to speak for God and handed out more desirable, optimistic news. But since the prophets' messages were from God, their predictions invariably proved to be correct.

THOSE WHO SPOKE FOR GOD WERE WILLING TO PAY THE PRICE. Some prophets were ridiculed by their contemporaries and threatened by priests and kings. Jeremiah, for example, was imprisoned, and the king burned scrolls containing his prophecies. The prophets' job was to confront those in the wrong with the words of God, and they would not be silenced.

930–586 BC
Kings of Judah rule

835–796 BC
Ministry of Joel

742–687 BC
Ministry of Micah

740–681 BC
Ministry of Isaiah

time Israel fell to the Assyrians and Assyria threatened Judah. Nahum and Zephaniah saw the impending defeat of the Assyrians but the growing threat of the Babylonians. Jeremiah and Habakkuk warned of the coming invasion of Judah by the Babylonians and promised that God would not abandon those who turned to him.

FOR REPENTANCE

DAILY READING PLAN

May 17: Joel 1
May 18: Micah 1; Isaiah 6
May 19: Nahum 1;
          Zephaniah 2:13-15
May 20: Jeremiah 1:4-19; 36
May 21: Habakkuk 1; 3:16-19

ITS PART IN GOD'S PLAN

The southern kingdom survived longer than the northern kingdom. But the presence of the temple in Jerusalem and superficial religious practices were not enough. God demanded obedience to the Law given to them by Moses. The prophets warned of the results of their disobedience.

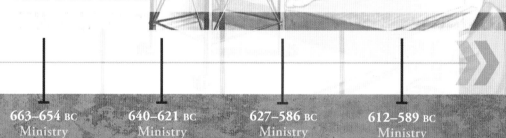

663–654 BC
Ministry
of Nahum

640–621 BC
Ministry
of Zephaniah

627–586 BC
Ministry
of Jeremiah

612–589 BC
Ministry
of Habakkuk

The message of many prophets transcended their immediate political situations. Those situations were just a warm-up for God's big event. God's purpose was never to form a permanent world power that would conquer other nations; it was to form a nation from which would come an eternal king who would rule an eternal,

When it happened...
835–586 BC

Where it happened...
Judah

PROPHETS ETERNAL

ITS PART IN GOD'S PLAN

From the time of Adam and Eve, the gulf between God and humankind has been unfathomable. Because of our rebellion, the ability to be like God or even understand God was beyond our grasp. Bit by bit, over centuries, God's prophets taught human beings about his plan. The prophets of Judah began to shed more and more light on God's plan for a coming eternal king and his eternal kingdom.

930–586 BC
Kings of
Judah rule

835–796 BC
Ministry
of Joel

international kingdom. *Joel spoke of a day when God's Spirit would live in all who called on him. Micah spoke of a king from Bethlehem who would rule an eternally peaceful kingdom. Isaiah promised a special servant who would pay the price for all who had turned from God.*

PREDICT AN KINGDOM

DAILY READING PLAN

May 22: Joel 2:28-32; Acts 2:14-24

May 23: Isaiah 7:2, 10-14; 8:11-17; 9:1-7

May 24: Isaiah 53

May 25: Micah 4:1-5; 5:2

May 26: Jeremiah 31:31-34; 33:14-16

MAJOR THEMES

THE PROMISED KING WOULD PAY THE PRICE ONCE AND FOR ALL. We would like peace with God. But we like to forget that we are the ones who started the war! The normal way of putting down an insurrection is for a powerful king to make the insurrectionists pay the price for their treason. But Isaiah began to tell of a coming king who would himself pay the penalty for sedition so humankind can have peace with God.

GOD WOULD ONE DAY LIVE WITHIN HIS PEOPLE RATHER THAN IN A TEMPLE. The ark of the covenant was a physical reminder that God is powerful and yet ultimately unapproachable by common people. But the prophets began to reveal that once the promised king made arrangements to remove the guilt from humankind, God would be more than approachable. Not only would people be able to approach God; he would actually live with them and *within* them!

GOD HAS ALWAYS WANTED A NATION COMPOSED OF ALL NATIONS. From the time of Babel, humankind was divided by language, ethnicity, and geography. The promised king would be the ruler of human beings from every language, ethnic group, and continent.

742–687 BC
Ministry
of Micah

740–681 BC
Ministry
of Isaiah

627–586 BC
Ministry
of Jeremiah

The Babylonian army surrounded the city of Jerusalem and laid siege to it. The military strategy of the siege was to surround a walled city, cutting off means of escape and disrupting supplies coming into it. When opposition was worn down by hunger, the attacking army would break through and conquer the city.

When it happened...
586 BC

Where it happened...
Jerusalem

DAILY READING PLAN

May 27: 2 Kings 25:1-21
May 28: 2 Chronicles 36:15-21
May 29: Jeremiah 39
May 30: Jeremiah 52

594 BC Solon institutes democratic reforms in Athens

The city wall, the temple, and the palace were burned and the wealth of the city plundered. A small number of the remaining Jews were taken to Babylon and lived as captives there.

FALL OF JERUSALEM

ITS PART IN GOD'S PLAN

The theme of this story is not that God is angry but that God is merciful. From the beginning of the Jewish nation, they were called to bless all nations. Instead, they sought only to bless themselves. The remnant of Judah would now be taken into the rest of the world, blessing their captors with the knowledge of the one true God.

<table>
<tr><td rowspan="3">MAJOR THEMES</td><td>GOD WILL JUDGE EVIL. The people of Judah had been warned. One prophet after another, over the course of three centuries, gave the same message. Unless the people of Judah returned to the Lord, he would judge. Jehovah was patient. But patience in judgment is not the same as leniency.</td></tr>
<tr><td>NOMINAL RELIGION DOES NOT SAVE. Some Jews surely believed that regardless of their behavior, they were safe. After all, they were part of the chosen nation, blood descendants of Abraham. But nominal adherence to a religion does not please God.</td></tr>
<tr><td>GOD'S PLAN WILL NOT BE THWARTED. Despite the disobedience of his people, God would continue to act. God could have totally destroyed the Jewish nation, and rightfully so. But he did not. He saved a remnant, a small portion of the nation. God's plan (including bringing the promised king who would redeem all people) would be fulfilled through them.</td></tr>
</table>

586 BC
Jerusalem falls to Babylon

551 BC Birth of Confucius

Nebuchadnezzar's army conquered Judah and sent Israelites into exile in Babylon. Only the poorest and most powerless remained to tend the fields of Israel. But God empowered prophets among his people in captivity to carry a message of warning as well as hope.

DANIEL AND PROPHETS IN

MAJOR THEMES

RECOGNIZE THE PROBLEM. A common mind-set among the grieving Jews was that the loss of their nation, the exile, was the fault of the wrongdoings of their ancestors; therefore, the nation would be quickly restored. Ezekiel warned the people to come to grips with their personal rebellion against God and not blame others in hopes of a quick resolution to their dire situation.

THE WORLD HAS ROOM FOR ONLY ONE KING. The Jews had gotten into trouble anytime they forgot that God was their true king. After their nation was destroyed, they began to understand a larger truth more clearly—God was not only the king of Israel but the king of the entire world as well. Daniel told Nebuchadnezzar that his kingdom would end, and it ended in Daniel's lifetime. God also promised that the next world power would fall (the Medo-Persian Empire), as would the one following that (the Greek Empire). He further predicted that in the day of a fourth world power (the Roman Empire), God himself would establish an eternal kingdom.

GOD WILL NOT BE CONTAINED. Ezekiel's vision of a stream flowing from the temple in Jerusalem contradicted the laws of nature—the stream grew wider and deeper the farther it flowed! That stream of God's Spirit would flow into the entire world, and his presence would be recognized everywhere. Whether by the waters of Babylon, inside a furnace, or in a den of lions, God was there.

DAILY READING PLAN

627–586 BC
Ministry of Jeremiah

c. 606–536 BC
Ministry of Daniel

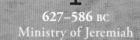

c. 605–562 BC Rule of Nebuchadnezzar and dominance of the Babylonian Empire

c. 550–330 BC Dominance of the Persian Empire (much of modern-day Iran)

When it happened...
c. 586–536 BC

Where it happened...
Babylon

EZEKIEL, EXILE

ITS PART IN GOD'S PLAN

The Babylonians could take the people of Israel out of their country, but they could not keep the God of that nation from his people! God's messages, spoken through Daniel and Ezekiel, corrected and encouraged the Jews—calling for spiritual rebirth and promising better days ahead. The remarkable work of God also became part of the history of Israel's captors, creating a hunger for the God of Israel in the people of the rest of the world.

593–571 BC
Ministry of Ezekiel

586 BC Jerusalem
falls to Babylon

334 BC Alexander the
Great invades Asia Minor
and defeats Persians,
Greek Empire expands

168 BC Rome defeats
Macedon, ensuring
dominance over Greece

Daniel and Ezekiel, Prophets in Exile · 99

The Babylonian Empire crumbled. The Persian Empire stood in its place. With the new empire came a new policy of religious tolerance. In his first year on the throne, Cyrus decreed that Jews who wished to return to their homeland were free to leave and

CYRUS OF

ITS PART IN GOD'S PLAN

God is in the business of restoration. Though he allowed the self-destructive actions of his people to lead to the inevitable results, he intervened. The temple would be rebuilt. More importantly, the nation would be gathered together again in the land given to Abraham.

538 BC King Cyrus of Persia issues a decree allowing Israelites to return to Jerusalem to rebuild the temple

c. 565 BC Spread of Taoism in China

c. 550 BC Earliest use of cast iron in China

rebuild the temple. He even arranged for the travel and construction to be properly financed! Under the leadership of Zerubbabel of the tribe of Judah, nearly fifty thousand people left Persia and headed for home. But much work lay before them.

PERSIA ENDS THE EXILE

When it happened...
538 BC

Where it happened...
Persia

DAILY READING PLAN

June 3: Isaiah 44:24–45:4; Jeremiah 25:12-14; Daniel 9:1-3

June 4: Ezra 1

MAJOR THEMES

GOD HAS A PLAN. Jeremiah had predicted an end to the exile within the span of a lifetime. Isaiah had predicted that a king named Cyrus would free his people from captivity. Such predictions seemed impossible because of the power of Babylon. But within the time frame foretold, Babylon fell and a Persian king named Cyrus rose to power.

GOD USES UNLIKELY SERVANTS. Cyrus did not worship the God of Abraham. But the Persians had a different view than the Assyrians and Babylonians concerning the religion of conquered lands. Instead of trying to destroy other religions, Cyrus sought to accommodate them. He attempted to please all the gods he could. And in doing so, he became an unwitting implement of the one true God.

GOD DOES NOT MIND REPEATING HIMSELF! In the days of Moses, God freed his people from bondage in Egypt. They did not leave empty-handed. The people of Egypt gave them precious materials that would be used to construct the tabernacle and its furnishings. Nine centuries later, God freed his people again, and they did not leave empty-handed! Cyrus ordered the citizens of his own empire to supply them with silver, gold, and other valuable gifts. Cyrus also returned gold and silver articles that had been taken by Babylon when Jerusalem fell.

c. 530 BC Greek mathematician Pythagoras of Samos develops his famous theorem

c. 520 BC Canal completed between the Nile River and Red Sea

The returning captives arrived in Jerusalem. They began their project by constructing the altar of sacrifice on its original site and starting to reinstate the offerings and festivals instituted by the Jewish Law. The laying of the foundation

REBUILDING

DAILY READING PLAN
June 5: Ezra 3
June 6: Ezra 4

When it happened...
536 BC

Where it happened...
Jerusalem

ITS PART IN GOD'S PLAN

Rebuilding the temple was no mere symbolic act. Temple worship differentiated between Judah and Israel. Temple practices performed by the priesthood bridged the gap between a holy God and a fallen people. The rebuilding of the temple promised a new beginning and hope for the fulfillment of God's promises.

585 BC Greek astronomer
Thales predicts an eclipse

Siddhartha Gautama
(Buddha, c. 563–483 BC)
founds Buddhism in India

was celebrated with praise and thanksgiving. But soon, opposition by those living in the land slowed progress. Eventually, after an order issued by Cyrus's successor, construction stopped completely.

OF THE
TEMPLE BEGINS

MAJOR THEMES

WITHOUT AN ALTAR, THERE IS NO PARTNERSHIP WITH GOD. Logic dictates that one builds a structure and then furnishes it. But Jeshua, his fellow priests, and Zerubbabel demanded a different course. Before the actual temple was restored, the altar of sacrifice was built. The priests reminded the people that the cost of treason had to be recognized before they could join with God in the construction of the entire temple.

OUR HAPPINESS IS AFFECTED BY WHETHER WE LIVE IN THE PAST OR THE FUTURE. When the foundation of the temple was laid, the people gathered for a time of worship and praise. But those who had seen the original temple wept when they compared the new foundation with the glory of the former temple of Solomon; younger people who had not known the first temple broke out in shouts of joy. Lessons of the past are important, but we must remember that the best days lie ahead for the children of God.

THE ENEMY WILL TRY TO KEEP GOD'S PEOPLE FROM FULFILLING THEIR MISSION. When the northern kingdom of Israel fell, citizens of the Assyrian Empire were brought in and were taught how to worship Jehovah. Instead of doing so faithfully, they mixed elements of the Law of Moses with their pagan religious practices. When the descendants of these people saw the temple being rebuilt, they first tried to compromise the project by taking partial ownership of it. When that did not work, they stooped to infiltration and subterfuge. Finally, they appealed to government authority to restrain the builders by force.

538 BC Zerubbabel leads exiles back to Jerusalem

536 BC Jews celebrate the laying of the temple's foundation

536–520 BC Opposition and fear stop the rebuilding project

Those traveling back to Jerusalem assumed great risk. Local bureaucrats could easily view the rebuilding of a crucial structure by a conquered nation as an act of rebellion. And that is exactly what happened. It is understandable that the

HAGGAI AND

DAILY READING PLAN

June 7: Ezra 5

June 8: Haggai 1

June 9: Zechariah 4

June 10: Haggai 2:6-9; Zechariah 14:20, 21

June 11: Ezra 6

MAJOR THEMES

GOD CAN EITHER PUSH OR PULL TO GET US MOVING IN HIS DIRECTION. To break the impasse caused by opposition to building the temple, God sent a team of prophets. Through Haggai, God pushed. Haggai's message was a straightforward scolding for putting personal comfort and safety before the mission to which the people were called. On the other hand, Zechariah pulled. His encouraging, mysterious, and poetic message gently led the people with a promise of hope and power from God's Spirit.

THE MISTAKES OF THE PAST WILL NOT PREVENT FUTURE SUCCESS. Nothing good comes from statements that begin with the words "If only you had not . . ." Implying that the future is irrevocably damaged from a mistake in the past is an accusation of the devil. Although the messages of Haggai and Zechariah differ in tone, both focus on the future. Haggai promised that the new temple would be more glorious than the old temple. Zechariah promised that even the most common implement in the new temple would be greater than the holiest implements of the old temple.

A WORD FROM GOD CAN GIVE COURAGE. The political situation did not change because of these prophecies. It was still dangerous to proceed. But the people did so anyway. God intervened by taking the request of those who accused the builders of wrongdoing and using it to get the king to authorize the building once more.

520–518 BC
Zechariah's ministry

c. 550 BC Carthage conquers
Sicily and Corsica

people's will to continue building the temple was taken away. But God called two prophets to energize and empower the people once more.

ZECHARIAH

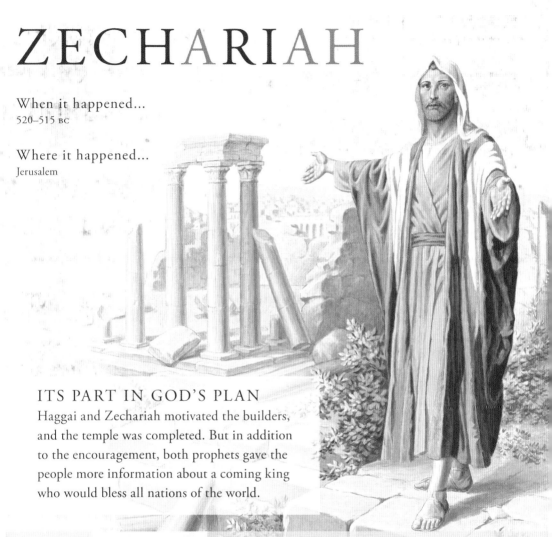

When it happened...
520–515 BC

Where it happened...
Jerusalem

ITS PART IN GOD'S PLAN

Haggai and Zechariah motivated the builders, and the temple was completed. But in addition to the encouragement, both prophets gave the people more information about a coming king who would bless all nations of the world.

520–515 BC
Haggai's ministry

c. 509 BC Rome becomes a republic

King Xerxes, apparently oblivious to the history of some of the people he ruled, chose an orphan Jewess to replace the deposed Queen Vashti. At about the same time, he appointed a prime minister whose people had a history of enmity with the Jews. Meanwhile, the cousin and foster father of the new queen exposed a plot to

ESTHER, JEWISH

OF

When it happened...
c. 485–474 BC

Where it happened...
Susa in Persia

ITS PART IN GOD'S PLAN
Most of Old Testament history to this point focused on the nation of Israel, but a great change was beginning to take place. While some Jews had returned to Jerusalem to rebuild the temple, God was working with others who remained in the land of exile.

486–465 BC
Reign of Xerxes the Great
(Ahasuerus), king of Persia

487 BC Egypt revolts
against the Persians

assassinate Xerxes and saved the king's life. When Prime Minister Haman devised a genocidal scheme, the stories of all these characters collided. Haman's plot was foiled, the Jewish heritage of Esther was revealed, and Mordecai was elevated to an influential political position.

QUEEN PERSIA

DAILY READING PLAN

June 12: Esther 1, 2
June 13: Esther 3
June 14: Esther 4, 5
June 15: Esther 6, 7
June 16: Esther 8–10

MAJOR THEMES

GOD IS ACTIVE EVEN WHEN HIS NAME IS NOT MENTIONED. Among the Bible books, Esther is unique—God is not mentioned. The heroine of the story is even cautioned to keep her Jewish heritage a secret! Nevertheless, God's work is evident. How else could an orphan of wartime captives become queen without a weapon being raised or a drop of blood being shed? How else could a day marked for slaughter become an ongoing holiday? How else could a people slated for genocide grow more powerful because of the plot against them? Not speaking God's name does not make him disappear!

IGNORING EVIL WILL EVENTUALLY CAUSE BIG PROBLEMS. Haman had a thousand-year-old chip on his shoulder. His ancestors, the Amalekites, had attacked the people of Israel without provocation when Moses was leading them out of Egypt. The Amalekites lost the battle, and this feud was never completely settled. More than ten centuries later Haman held the political power to destroy all Jews.

SERVING GOD DEMANDS BOLD ACTION. Throughout the history of Israel, God would miraculously bring someone into a position of power. But time after time, those leaders tried to preserve that power through caution, compromise, or coalitions with other political forces. When Esther hesitated to use her power decisively, Mordecai reminded her that she was not placed in power to be comfortable but to be courageous.

Sometime between 485–474 BC
Queen Esther of Persia intervenes for her Jewish people

464–424 BC Reign of Artaxerxes I (son of Xerxes), king of Persia

460 BC Cincinnatus rises to power in Rome

To this day, the festival of Purim celebrates for Jewish people the deliverance recorded in the book of Esther

During the reign of Artaxerxes I, a second group of exiles returned to Israel, led by Ezra, a descendant of Aaron (Israel's first high priest). Shortly thereafter, word came to Nehemiah, who was serving in Artaxerxes' court, that the walls of Jerusalem

EZRA AND
FOR A

When it happened...
c. 457–440 BC

Where it happened...
Jerusalem

DAILY READING PLAN

June 17: Ezra 7
June 18: Ezra 9
June 19: Nehemiah 1
June 20: Nehemiah 2, 3
June 21: Nehemiah 8, 9, 13

ITS PART IN GOD'S PLAN

In some Jewish traditions, the time of Ezra and Nehemiah is referred to as a new springtime in Israel. Ezra is credited with reviving Jewish worship, encouraging study of the Law of Moses, and even assembling the writings of the prophets into the collection of books we know as the Hebrew Bible, or Old Testament. Knowledge of the past would be crucial for the great event God had planned for the future.

c. 457 BC Ezra leads a group of Jews back to Israel from exile

c. 470 BC Greek philosopher Socrates is born

had not been rebuilt and the city was unprotected. Nehemiah was granted permission by the king to supervise the rebuilding of the walls. Together, Ezra and Nehemiah restored moral and civil order to Israel.

NEHEMIAH CALL FRESH START

MAJOR THEMES

RELIGIOUS AUTHORITY AND CIVIL AUTHORITY ARE BOTH VITAL TO A NATION. Throughout the history of the Jews, a strict separation between the roles of priest and king was maintained. This continued during the time of Ezra and Nehemiah. The books of Ezra and Nehemiah are one story, but the two main characters are rarely described as interacting. Ezra focused on the temple and religious observances, while Nehemiah focused on the protective city walls and civil leadership. But their accomplishments mesh seamlessly. When threatened by opposition, those rebuilding the walls both prayed and posted a guard!

GOD'S WORD INSPIRES CONTRADICTORY EMOTIONS. When Ezra returned to Israel, he was heartbroken to find that his countrymen continued to violate the laws, especially those concerning intermarriage with people who did not worship the God of Abraham. Ezra later gathered the people and read the words recorded by Moses centuries before. Their first reaction was to mourn how far short they'd fallen before a holy God. But Ezra and Nehemiah instructed them to celebrate. Though they had forgotten God's commands, God had continued to remember them and desired a relationship with them.

GOD PAINTS ON A WIDE CANVAS. Why would a pagan king allow another group of subjects to return to their homeland? Why would that king send his servant to supervise the refortification of their capital city? We must remember how God had already worked in both Jerusalem and Persia. Queen Esther was Artaxerxes' stepmother. He had been reared during the time when Mordecai rose to prominence. It is not hard to imagine that Artaxerxes had an extensive knowledge of the people of Israel that informed his decisions.

c. 445 BC Nehemiah goes to Jerusalem and rebuilds the city walls

c. 300 BC Zeno of Citium founds Stoicism in Athens

The temple was rebuilt, allowing worship in accordance to the Law of Moses. Jerusalem was refortified, allowing a measure of political security. But even though Israel had been confronted about the behavior that led to their exile,

MALACHI, THE TESTAMENT

MAJOR THEMES

GOD MUST HAVE PRIORITY IN OUR FINANCES. In the days of Joshua, God commanded that land be given to the descendants of every son of Jacob but one. The Levites were to care for the tabernacle (and later, the temple) and supervise the sacrificial system set up by God through Moses. They were provided for by many of the gifts brought to the temple. But after the exiles returned, the temple was built, Jerusalem was secured, and people settled into the routine of everyday life, money was tight. Some skipped offering certain sacrifices or tried to substitute defective animals that were of no use. This threatened the livelihood of the Levites and the future of temple worship. But more than anything, it was a statement that the people did not trust God to meet their needs.

GOD MUST HAVE PRIORITY IN OUR RELATIONSHIPS. The Law of Moses allowed for divorce. But many exiles were abusing that provision. The difficult life of rebuilding a country would certainly have taken its toll on physical beauty. Apparently, some Jewish men were divorcing their wives to marry younger women in the area. This was a violation of God's commands not to marry women who worshiped other gods. But it was also a violation of the sacred covenant of marriage.

GOD MUST SHAPE OUR PLANS FOR THE FUTURE. The final words of the last Old Testament prophet were not of doom. Malachi promised a time in which a new day of righteousness would dawn and the fame of God would reach far beyond their borders. God still wants his people to anticipate the Day of the Lord with joy, not fear.

c. 455 BC Anaxagoras teaches that the world is created with small, orderly particles (atoms)

c. 450 BC Reindeer domesticated in central Asia

many continued to ignore the commands of God. Malachi clearly warned that ignoring God was a dangerous game. But he also promised that God would reward those who remained faithful to him.

FINAL OLD PROPHET

When it happened...
c. 430 BC

Where it happened...
Jerusalem

ITS PART IN GOD'S PLAN

God's message was revealed over a period of centuries. Each generation learned more and more about what God required and what he was planning. Through the time of Malachi, God had counseled his people to follow his commands and have the life he intended for them. But they demonstrated the same spirit of rebellion as Adam and Eve. What else could God say? Israel would have to wait four hundred years to find out.

DAILY READING PLAN
June 22: Malachi 2:10-16; 3:6-12; 4

c. 430 BC
Ministry of Malachi

385 BC Plato establishes his Academy

Aristotle (384–322 BC) teaches

The Jews had long received messages that had divine authority and were to be recorded in writing, preserved for future generations. But for four hundred years those prophetic messages stopped. God's people reacted to this famine of the Word of God in the same way that people react to a famine of food—they protected, treasured, and savored

FOUR CENTURIES

ITS PART IN GOD'S PLAN

This period without a prophetic word from God allowed time for the Law and the writings of the prophets to be preserved. During this time those writings were studied, applied, and passed along to people outside the Jewish community.

DAILY READING PLAN

June 23: Amos 8:11; Nehemiah 12:27, 31-36; Luke 7:1-5; Acts 10:1, 2; 13:42, 43

When it happened...
430 BC–AD 25

Where it happened...
Throughout the known world

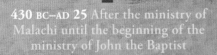

430 BC–AD 25 After the ministry of Malachi until the beginning of the ministry of John the Baptist

c. 330 BC Alexander the Great conquers Persian Empire

every morsel they had. During this period, the office of scribe came into prominence. Scribes copied, collected, and protected what we now know as the Old Testament. Other scribes wrote commentaries and extrapolations based on the Scriptures. Synagogues were built all over the known world for the study of the written Word of God.

WITHOUT A PROPHET

THE WORDS OF GOD ARE PRECIOUS. After the time of Ezra, the Jews adopted very strict regulations concerning the copying of the Law of Moses and the writings of the prophets. Only approved animal skins and a specific formulation of ink could be used. Scribes had to speak the words aloud as they copied them. Scrolls containing the Scriptures were securely stored and could not be destroyed. The ancient words were reproduced with astounding accuracy, and the scrolls containing them lasted for generations.

STUDYING GOD'S WORD IS A GOOD REASON TO MEET WITH OTHERS. As regional rulers allowed, meeting places called synagogues (meaning "a gathering," or "assembly") were constructed. Sometimes local residents who were not descendants of Abraham attended. These "devout men," as some writers called them, were drawn to hear the written Word of God taught.

ANCIENT WORDS HAVE MODERN APPLICATION. The words of respected teachers of the Scriptures were gathered. This commentary, once only handed down from generation to generation orally, was recorded in written form and called the Mishnah (meaning "repetition," or "review"). Books of moral teaching, commentary, and history were also written and studied. These books, called the Apocrypha ("hidden books") by Protestant churches and Deutero-canonicals ("second regulations") by Orthodox churches, are recognized as Scripture by Orthodox churches but are considered helpful, though not authoritative, by Jews and Protestants today.

c. 300–200 BC Synagogues in Egypt known to exist

164–63 BC The Jews revolt under the Maccabees and take back control of Israel

c. 63 BC Roman general Pompey conquers Jerusalem

Although God sent no prophets for four centuries, he made sure that a number of preparations were made for the coming of the promised eternal king. During the reign of the Persians, some of the works of God on behalf of his people became parts of government records and were widely distributed. During the Greek reign,

GOD PREPARES AN

When it happened...
430 BC–AD 25

Where it happened...
Throughout the known world

DAILY READING PLAN
June 24: Daniel 3:28-30; 6:25-28
June 25: Esther 10
June 26: Ezra 1:1, 4; 6:1-12

ITS PART IN GOD'S PLAN
While the Jews were preserving and studying the words of the prophets, the rest of the world was studying the people of God! A common language and a highway system also set the stage to allow the whole world to listen the next time God spoke.

430 BC–AD 25 During the time after Malachi and before John the Baptist, Persian records document God's works

Sometime between 356–323 BC Greek becomes the lingua franca (common language) of the Mediterranean area *a common language came into use throughout the known world, and the Hebrew Scriptures were even translated into Greek. During Roman rule, a system of roads and a military presence helped make overland transportation relatively available and secure.*

THE WORLD FOR ETERNAL KING

THE WORLD WILL NOTICE WHEN GOD ACTS. Nebuchadnezzar of Babylon forbade his subjects from blaspheming the God of Daniel's friends Shadrach, Meshach, and Abednego. After Daniel escaped the lions, Darius the Mede demanded that all his subjects revere the God of Daniel. During the return of the Jews to Jerusalem, Persian kings sent out official proclamations concerning the Jews and their God. After the events recorded in the book of Esther, Xerxes of Persia saw that the works of Mordecai were a part of the official record. Although the Jews were a captive people, the secular world spread the word about the God of the Jews.

THE WORLD WILL TALK ABOUT GOD WHEN IT HAS THE LANGUAGE TO DO SO. After Alexander the Great established the Greek Empire, Greek became the common language of the day. Tradition teaches that the Greek king of Egypt, Ptolemy II Philadelphus, ordered that the Jewish Scriptures be translated from Hebrew to Greek for inclusion in the famous Library of Alexandria. The proliferation of synagogues during the same time was another factor that enabled people throughout the known world to hear the Word of God read and taught.

GOD CAN USE PREPARATIONS OF WAR FOR BRINGING HIS PEACE. The Roman army depended on the use of bases in which to prepare for battle, refresh and reequip troops, and keep a large number of soldiers waiting for the opportunity to strike. And the bases needed to be connected by good roads for easy access and supply from Rome. Ironically, the network of roads created for military dominance would become the thoroughfares by which God's new covenant message would be delivered to the entire world.

312 BC Construction of the Appian Way, the most famous of the Roman roads, begins

c. 280–132 BC Hebrew Scriptures translated into Greek (Septuagint)

THE BIRTH OF JOHN THE BAPTIST

MAJOR THEMES

GOD IS THE GOD OF THE PRESENT, THE PAST, AND FOREVER. The story of God's new covenant began in a way very similar to the story of God's old covenant: God promised an aging, infertile couple a son. The comparison of Zechariah and Elizabeth to Abram and Sarai was intentional. It was a sign that God was about to change the world once more.

SOMETIMES WE NEED TO BE QUIET WHILE GOD WORKS. God's story of restoring humankind is filled with ironic humor. Zechariah was a priest authorized to come to God on behalf of the people. He knew God heard and answered prayers. He knew his nation began when God promised an infertile couple a son. Then the angel Gabriel appeared and told him his prayer had been heard and that he would father a son. How did Zechariah respond? He asked the angel how he could believe such a thing! This priest had plenty of time to reconsider his question. God made him unable to speak until the promise was fulfilled.

GOD'S PLAN IS BASED ON HIS GRACIOUSNESS. When Gabriel told Zechariah that he would father a son, he also told Zechariah what to name the child. This caused some confusion since the chosen name was not a family name. But the name was given for a purpose. *John* means "Yahweh/Jehovah is gracious." John would be an outspoken prophet whose message would certainly rile many. But the gist of his message would be contained in his name: the God of grace had a plan for his people.

ITS PART IN GOD'S PLAN

The last words of the last Old Testament prophet predicted the coming of another prophet comparable to Elijah. From the time of John's birth, it was obvious that God was working in his life, and word spread. John would not be the promised king but the priest who would open the door between God and his people and make way for that king.

c. 100 BC Chinese develop the use of paper

51 BC Cleopatra assumes Egyptian throne

The angel Gabriel visited a priest named Zechariah while he was offering prayers for the people. Even though Zechariah and his wife, Elizabeth, were elderly and childless, Gabriel promised they would have a son and instructed them to name him John. Zechariah was unable to speak during his wife's pregnancy, but his first words after the birth of his son were to affirm the angel's message and praise God for allowing him to father the first prophet in Israel since Malachi.

DAILY READING PLAN

June 27: Malachi 4:5; Luke 1:5-25
June 28: Luke 1:57-80

When it happened...
Sometime between 6–5 BC

Where it happened...
Jerusalem

Sometime between
6–5 BC
Gabriel appears
to Zechariah

Sometime between
6–5 BC
Birth of John
the Baptist

44 BC Assassination of
Julius Caesar

In the sixth month of Elizabeth's pregnancy, Gabriel appeared to Mary of Nazareth. Mary visited her relative Elizabeth for three months and then returned to a surprised Joseph to whom she was engaged. About six months later, Joseph and Mary traveled

THE BIRTH OF

DAILY READING PLAN

June 29: Luke 1:26-56
June 30: Matthew 1:18-25
July 1: Luke 2:1-38
July 2: Matthew 2;
Luke 2:39, 40

When it happened...
Sometime between 6–4 BC

Where it happened...
Bethlehem

Sometime between 6–4 BC
Birth of Jesus,
angels announce Jesus'
birth to shepherds

37 BC Herod the Great becomes the king of Judea

27 BC Octavian (Julius Caesar's great-nephew) is given the title Caesar Augustus

to Bethlehem to be counted in a Roman census. They stayed in Bethlehem after Jesus' birth, but fled to Egypt when they learned that Herod planned to kill him. They did not return to take up residence in Nazareth until after the death of Herod.

JESUS

ITS PART IN GOD'S PLAN

The day God had planned from the beginning had come. Every detail had been prepared, leaving no doubt that the birth of this king was a unique act of God.

MAJOR THEMES

JESUS WAS BORN TO BE A KING LIKE NO OTHER. In the past, God intervened to give infertile couples a child. In the case of Jesus, God gave a child to a woman who had not had sexual intercourse! The prophet Isaiah had predicted this virgin birth centuries earlier. Jesus differed in another way from kings who preceded him. The offices of priest and king were kept separate throughout Israel's history. Yet since we know that Mary was related to Elizabeth, a direct descendant of Aaron the priest, Jesus was born from both the royal and the priestly lines. He would be both a priest and a king!

JESUS WAS BORN TO BE THE KING OF THE OUTCASTS. One would expect a king to be born in a palace surrounded by royalty. Jesus, however, was born in a stable. The first to learn of his birth were not princes, but paupers. Shepherds were not held in high esteem in first-century culture. Throughout Jesus' life he would continue to be the king of those who least deserved royal treatment!

JESUS WAS BORN TO BE KING OF ALL KINGDOMS. The child Jesus would have more visitors. The magi, astrologers from lands east of Judea, interpreted a star in the sky as a sign of the birth of a great king. Ironically, those who practiced pagan religions were the first to tell the religious leaders of the Jews about Jesus' birth! While Jesus was born to be king of the Jews, his kingdom would be open to people of every language, tribe, and nation.

Sometime between 6–4 BC
Visit of the magi

Sometime between 6–4 BC
Herod's slaughter of the innocents

4 BC Death of Herod the Great

When Jesus was twelve years old, he and his family traveled to Jerusalem to observe the Passover. Presumably they traveled with many others who made that regular pilgrimage. On the way home, Mary and Joseph discovered that Jesus

JESUS AT THE

DAILY READING PLAN
July 3: Luke 2:41-52
July 4: Hebrews 2:14-18; 4:14-16

JESUS WAS JEWISH. After Adam and Eve, the gulf between God and humankind was unimaginably great. God began to bridge that gap through Abraham—one nation was created to reveal to the rest of the world the nature and plan of God. The Jewish nation would also be the source of the completed revelation of God—a king who would actually be God in the flesh. As that king, Jesus was reared Jewish, following the Law of Moses. His family would celebrate the prescribed Jewish festivals, including the Passover. He was trained to read and understand the Law and the words of the prophets.

JESUS WAS DIVINE. At twelve, Jesus assumed adult responsibilities. So on this first pilgrimage to the temple, he would have been able to travel with the men rather than under the care of his mother. This was probably the reason Jesus was not missed for three days; each parent assumed he was with the other. Upon returning to the temple, they recognized the reason for his absence. Jesus was discussing his true Father's Word with the teachers there. His understanding amazed everyone who heard him. Exactly what was being discussed is not known for certain, but the time of Passover would have been a time to discuss God's ultimate sacrifice, the Lamb of God, who would cause death to pass over all who accepted him.

JESUS WAS ALSO A HUMAN BEING. Jesus was not an adult in a child's body. He developed physically, mentally, spiritually, and socially, as do all human beings. Jesus experienced every type of struggle that is common to all people.

c. 30 BC Sundials used in China

c. 28 BC Chinese astronomers discover sunspots

was missing. Backtracking to the temple, they found him discussing the Word of God with the teachers there. Jesus and his family returned home to Nazareth, where Jesus grew up.

AGE OF TWELVE

When it happened...
AD 8

Where it happened...
Jerusalem

ITS PART IN GOD'S PLAN

We know nothing of Jesus' childhood save this short account. But from it we learn that Jesus fully experienced the human condition while at the same time having a unique relationship with his Father in Heaven.

AD **8** Jesus asks and answers questions at the temple at age 12

AD **9** Germans ambush three Roman legions at Teutoburg Forest

AD **14** Augustus Caesar dies and Tiberius Caesar takes his place

The silence of God was broken. Four centuries after Malachi, a new prophet, John the son of Zechariah, spoke the Word of the Lord. As was typical of Hebrew prophets, John used a visual method to proclaim that message. His divinely mandated method was water baptism. At that time, the Jews employed water baptism when a Gentile (non-Jew) converted to Judaism. It aptly symbolized the removal of the moral filth

THE MINISTRY

ITS PART IN GOD'S PLAN

John was the opening act in God's drama of redemption through Jesus the Christ. John is the one the Old Testament prophets predicted would prepare the way for the coming Messiah. John was quick to recognize that his status was far lower than that of Jesus and that his popularity was to decrease while the popularity of Jesus increased.

When it happened...
c. AD 25–27

Where it happened...
Desert region near the Jordan River

AD 19 Death of Roman poet Virgil

of paganism. The scandal of John's baptism was that he required it of Jews, in effect saying that Jews were as morally reprehensible to God as were Gentiles. Predictably, the arrival of John excited the masses but angered the religious establishment. John's message was also aimed at the political establishment, a move that would lead to his imprisonment and execution.

OF JOHN THE BAPTIST

DAILY READING PLAN

July 5: Isaiah 40:1-5; Matthew 17:10-13
July 6: Matthew 3:1-12; Mark 1:1-8; Luke 3:1-20
July 7: John 1:19-28; 3:22-36

MAJOR THEMES

THE BEGINNING OF THE END IS HERE. The idea of the end times has always excited believers. But the last days were introduced when John testified of the presence of the Messiah. God's final transaction (or covenant, testament) with humankind is not just a future final judgment. It is the promise of salvation for all through the work of the Son of God.

SALVATION HAS TWO ESSENTIAL ELEMENTS. Wash a pig if you want, but it will immediately go back into the mud. For a pig to remain clean, it needs to stop being a pig! John taught that repentance and cleansing from sin were necessary to please God. He also taught that unless the nature of human beings changed, we would return to sin. The one who would baptize with the Holy Spirit, changing the inner nature of human beings, must come in order for salvation to be complete.

SALVATION IS FOR ALL. Everyone believes repentance is necessary. But we often believe it is necessary only for someone else! John dared teach that salvation would be for all, but that all—the religious and the irreligious, the powerful and powerless—had to admit their sinful state.

c. AD 25–27
Ministry of
John the Baptist

AD 43 Roman conquest
of Britain

John taught that all people needed to be cleansed from their wrongdoing. But he also taught that someone had come to complete the job of restoring humankind to God. He identified Jesus as that Savior. When John baptized Jesus, God confirmed the testimony

JESUS' BAPTISM

DAILY READING PLAN

July 8: Matthew 3:13-17;
Mark 1:9-11;
Luke 3:21, 22

July 9: Matthew 4:1-11;
Mark 1:12, 13;
Luke 4:1-13

When it happened...
AD 26

Where it happened...
The Jordan River and the
Judean Desert

AD **26** John baptizes
Jesus in the Jordan
River

AD **26** Satan
tempts Jesus
in the wilderness

AD **30** Christian baptism for
forgiveness and the gift of
the Holy Spirit initiated

Sometime between AD **100–150**
An early nonbiblical Christian
book, the Didache, gives instructions concerning baptism.

of John both visually and audibly. Then the Holy Spirit led Jesus into the wilderness for forty days of fasting. During that time Satan attempted to turn Jesus from his mission. Although the devil's attacks were ruthless, his tactics were successfully resisted.

AND TEMPTATION

ITS PART IN GOD'S PLAN

As it is said, every journey starts with a single step. Jesus' journey to the cross began with his baptism and his subsequent temptation. Once Jesus started his ministry, the bell could not be "unrung." The course was set for a ministry that would end in his death.

MAJOR THEMES

JESUS' IDENTITY WAS MADE CLEAR FROM THE BEGINNING. John the Baptist identified Jesus as the Lamb of God who would take away the sins of the world and who would allow for human nature to be changed through the indwelling of God's Holy Spirit. But according to the Law of Moses, testimony about someone must be given by two or three witnesses. At Jesus' baptism, John's words were confirmed when the Holy Spirit in the form of a dove alighted on Jesus and an audible voice from Heaven declared him to be the Son of God. There could be no doubt as to who Jesus was!

JESUS' TEMPTATIONS WERE VERY SIMILAR TO OURS. Being the Lamb of God meant two things. First, the sacrificial Passover lamb had to be without flaw; Jesus must live a sinless life. Second, in order to pay the debt caused by sin, the sacrifice had to die. As Jesus contemplated his ministry with a time of fasting, Satan attempted to keep him from beginning his task. He appealed to Jesus' physical appetites. He appealed to Jesus' belief in God's love and willingness to protect him. He appealed to Jesus' pride and desire for control. But Jesus resisted these familiar temptations by referring to the recorded Word of God.

SATAN DOES NOT GIVE UP. Jesus successfully resisted Satan's attacks. But this would not be the last time he would have to make a decision to do God's will rather than succumb to his own desires, fears, and pride. There would be another opportune time for the devil to tempt him some three years later.

JAAZIEL

Early in Jesus' ministry, he traveled from Jerusalem to Galilee. Although it was typical for Jews to go miles out of their way to avoid Samaria, Jesus did not. When his disciples went into a nearby town to buy food, Jesus approached a

SAMARITAN

DAILY READING PLAN

July 10: John 4:1-42
July 11: John 4:43-54
July 12: Mark 4:26-32

ITS PART IN GOD'S PLAN

Sometimes before we can get up, we need to recognize how far we have fallen. The first people to see the infant Jesus were despised shepherds. The first person to lead a successful evangelistic campaign was a woman of questionable character and of a reviled race. Jesus would continue to reach beyond borders and barriers to bring people to himself.

c. 1385 BC The bones of Joseph, son of Jacob, buried at Shechem

From 722 BC Northern kingdom of Israel conquered and inhabited by Assyrians. Intermarriage produces the mixed race known as the Samaritans.

Samaritan woman who was drawing water from a well. This led to a conversation that convinced the woman that Jesus was the Messiah. She ran back to her town and led others to meet Jesus.

WOMAN AT THE WELL

When it happened...
AD 26 or 27

Where it happened...
Near Sychar (Shechem of the Old Testament) in Samaria

MAJOR THEMES

JESUS CAN USE IMPERFECT PEOPLE. Centuries earlier when Israel was about to invade Jericho, one woman asked to be saved from the judgment her city would face. Rahab was a prostitute, but because of her faith she and her entire family escaped harm. In a strikingly similar event, Jesus met an outcast from a land where Jews saw even the most upright to be beneath contempt. Like Rahab, this unnamed woman wanted to be a part of what God was doing and to bring others along to join her.

ETHNIC AND GEOGRAPHICAL CONFLICTS ARE IRRELEVANT BECAUSE OF JESUS. Ever since Jeroboam I led the northern tribes of Israel in revolt and established new temples and a new priesthood, the question of a proper place of worship was a bone of contention between Judea and Samaria. This woman was convinced that Jesus was a prophet and, therefore, a logical person to settle the matter. Jesus affirmed that the temple in Jerusalem was authorized for worship in a way no other place could be. But he also pointed to the time when all believers would be united by the Holy Spirit to *become* the temple of God.

A DECISION TO FOLLOW JESUS CANNOT BE MADE FOR US. Their interest piqued by the woman's account of her encounter with Jesus, many townspeople returned with her to meet him, then urged him to stay two more days for an extended time of teaching. The testimony of the woman stirred their curiosity, but they needed to investigate Jesus' teachings firsthand in order to believe.

AD **26 or 27** Jesus meets a woman at the well in Sychar

Some disciples of John the Baptist became the first disciples of Jesus. They followed him from Judea, up to Cana in Galilee, and back to Jerusalem, before going back home to Galilee. But when the time came for a more

FISHERS OF MEN

When it happened...
Sometime between AD 26–27

Where it happened...
The shores of the Sea of Galilee

DAILY READING PLAN

July 13: John 1:35-51
July 14: Matthew 4:18-22; Mark 1:16-20
July 15: Luke 5:1-11

Sometime between AD 26–27
Some disciples of John the
Baptist follow Jesus

Before recorded history
Ancient men make fish-
hooks out of bone

GREGORIOSZ

Before recorded history
Ancient Serbian settlement
of Lepenski Vir uses fishing
as a major food source

extensive ministry campaign throughout Galilee, these disciples quickly responded to Jesus' call. Peter, Andrew, James, and John dropped their nets and left their boats to begin an adventure that had no equal.

WE NEED TO ACT ON WHAT WE KNOW. John the Baptist identified Jesus as the Lamb of God who would take away the sins of the world. For that reason, some of John's disciples began to follow Jesus. Andrew told his brother Simon Peter about Jesus. Philip found Nathanael and told him. As these early followers of John learned more about the coming Messiah, they acted on what they knew by seeking Jesus and bringing others to him.

JESUS SPEAKS OUR LANGUAGE. Fishermen were among Jesus' first disciples. Jesus did not immediately begin a deep, scholarly discourse about God's plans. Instead, he spoke "fisherman." Jesus described the mission of spreading his message to others as being "fishers of men." He illustrated that metaphor with an unforgettable miracle. After Peter had spent a fruitless night on the job, Jesus set out with him again. In moments, his nets were overflowing. Undoubtedly that image was remembered for a lifetime!

WE HAVE ONE VOCATION. Apparently, some of Jesus' first disciples spent a short time with Jesus in Judea before returning to their full-time jobs as fishermen. But when Jesus called Peter, Andrew, James, and John from their boats to a long-term commitment, they quickly agreed. We all have different avocations—interests, hobbies, and jobs. But believers in Christ have one vocation, or life's calling: to reach the world with the message of Jesus.

ITS PART IN GOD'S PLAN

Jesus was the promised king. So who were his "princes" and "generals"? Hardly what one would expect! Jesus began his ministry with very simple, uneducated men. They added nothing to him. He was the one who would shape this ragtag bunch into a band that would literally change the course of human civilization.

Sometime between AD 26–27 Jesus calls his first disciples to join him on an extensive ministry campaign in Galilee

c. AD 100 Moche people of ancient Peru depict fishermen in their ceramics

c. AD 180 Greek author Oppian of Corycus writes a major treatise on fishing

Jesus continued to collect his inner circle of disciples during three campaigns through Galilee. At the end of that time, Jesus would send his chosen twelve out on their own to preach to their fellow Jews. Matthew (also called Levi) must

MATTHEW, THE

DAILY READING PLAN

July 16: Matthew 9:9-13; Mark 2:13-17; Luke 5:27-32
July 17: Matthew 10
July 18: Luke 15; 19:1-10

MAJOR THEMES

JESUS FORGIVES THE UNFORGIVABLE. Jesus accepted those shunned by society because of their social status or national heritage. But Matthew's case was totally different. Tax collectors chose to cooperate with the occupying forces of Rome, taking money from their countrymen to fill the coffers of the enemy. Furthermore, the tax collector would extort more than the amount required in order to enrich himself. Matthew was not merely someone born in poverty or of another race. He was someone who chose a traitorous and self-serving lifestyle. Yet Jesus not only offered Matthew forgiveness; he invited him to join his inner circle!

FORGIVENESS IS OFFENSIVE TO THE SELF-RIGHTEOUS. No one can meet God's holy standards by his or her own efforts. Yet those who believe they can are offended when someone whom they consider beneath them is accepted and forgiven. Matthew accepted forgiveness and invited his friends to share a meal with Jesus. This was nothing short of scandalous to the Pharisees, the sect of Judaism that prided itself on strict adherence to the Law of Moses.

FORGIVENESS BRINGS UNITY AMONG THE FORGIVEN. Matthew's fellow Jews would have considered him to be a traitor. But one party of the Jews went even further. The Zealots believed that political assassination was an appropriate response to Roman occupation and those who aided it. Yet Matthew joined the group of Jesus' disciples that included a forgiven Simon the Zealot! Those who are forgiven can risk forgiving others.

c. 1886 BC Joseph, son of Jacob, authorizes taxes on grain harvested in the years before a famine in Egypt

c. 3000 BC Oldest known system of taxation in Egypt

c. 300 BC Taxation of salt during the Mauryan Empire in India

have been a controversial choice. Tax collectors were despised for good reasons. Yet Jesus invited Matthew to join him, and in response Matthew closed up shop for good.

TAX COLLECTOR

When it happened...
AD 27

Where it happened...
Galilee

ITS PART IN GOD'S PLAN

As a tax collector, Matthew must have been able to read and write, possibly in three languages. Matthew not only joined the disciples but also is credited with later writing one of the four Gospels. Interestingly enough, it is Matthew's Gospel that has recorded more of Jesus' long sermons and series of parables than any of the others.

AD **27** Jesus calls Matthew, also known as Levi, to be his disciple

AD **29** Jesus sends his 12 disciples to preach to their fellow Jews

AD **30** Jesus forgives Zacchaeus, a chief tax collector from Jericho

c. 49 BC Julius Caesar imposes 1 percent sales tax in Rome

After three campaigns on the western side of the Sea of Galilee, Jesus ordered his disciples to cross the sea into predominantly Gentile territory. As they crossed, a storm arose, nearly capsizing their vessel. They awoke Jesus, who was sleeping in the boat, and he commanded the wind and waves to stop. The response was immediate.

CALMING THE

MAJOR THEMES

FEAR CAN RESULT WHEN WE ARE UNSURE OF THE FUTURE. It is possible that the disciples were fearful long before the storm arose. Jesus had set their course for the eastern side of the Sea of Galilee. Up to this point, Jesus sent the twelve among the Jews. But at their new destination they would encounter those who raised pigs, a ceremonially unclean animal according to Jewish law. What else might they find there?

FEAR CAN RESULT WHEN WE ARE NOT SURE WE ARE LOVED. If they did fear going into the territory of non-Jews, the sudden storm might have served to confirm their fears. Was God judging them for venturing that far? When these experienced fishermen found their boat nearly capsizing and Jesus sleeping, they questioned his love for them.

GOING THROUGH A STORM WITH JESUS SHOWS WHO HE IS AND HOW MUCH HE LOVES US. The disciples feared for their lives one moment and found themselves on a totally calm sea seconds later. They asked each other a rhetorical question: What kind of man can do something like this? The answer was obvious. Jesus had the power to command them into unknown difficulties and had the love to protect them on the journey.

ITS PART IN GOD'S PLAN

Most if not all the disciples had been with Jesus about two years at this point. They had seen great miracles, but they had yet to see the full extent of who he was. When they reached the shore, they encountered the alarming sight of demon-possessed men in a graveyard. Certainly the power demonstrated by Jesus the night before assured them in this new frightening encounter.

AD **29**
Jesus stills a storm
on the Sea of Galilee

DAILY READING PLAN

July 19: Matthew 8:23-27; Mark 4:35-41; Luke 8:22-25
July 20: Matthew 8:28-34; Mark 5:1-17; Luke 8:26-37
July 21: Matthew 14:22-36; Mark 6:45-51; John 6:15-21

STORM

When it happened...
AD 29

Where it happened...
Sea of Galilee

AD 29
Jesus orders demons
into a herd of pigs

AD 29
Jesus walks on water

Jesus left Galilee to go to Jerusalem for one of the festivals commanded by Jewish law. During that time he visited a pool near one of the city gates. Because the pool was rumored to have healing properties, a number of people with severe disabilities

BETHESDA POOL

When it happened...
c. AD 29

Where it happened...
Jerusalem

c. AD 29
Jesus heals the man
at Bethesda Pool

For centuries people have gone to mineral springs for supposed therapeutic value:

Lithium springs, such as those in Oregon's Lithia Park, are said to enhance mood.

spent their days there, hoping for a miraculous healing. Jesus spoke with a man who had been disabled for nearly four decades—and instantly healed him. But since the miracle took place on a Sabbath Day, it drew the attention of the religious authorities.

DAILY READING PLAN

July 22: John 5:1-15
July 23: John 7:37-44
July 24: John 9

MAJOR THEMES

CODEPENDENCE CAN BE COMFORTABLE! Though the man at the pool had suffered for many years, he continued to spend his days in the company of others who suffered there. He seems to show that misery does indeed love company, and it appears that he may have grown comfortable in his misery! Jesus centered in on the problem and asked the man if he really wanted to get well.

GOD WILL NOT FORCE HIS WILL ON US. The power to heal came from Jesus. But time after time, Jesus asked those who were suffering to make some show of trust as a part of that healing. In this case, Jesus simply asked the man to take the mat he was lying on and get up. Jesus did the rest!

PEOPLE ARE MORE IMPORTANT THAN RITUAL. There is a humor in legalism that seems to be lost on the legalistic. A man had been disabled for thirty-eight years. When legalists saw him carrying his bedroll, they did not rejoice in his healing. Rather they scolded him for carrying a burden on a day on which work was forbidden.

ITS PART IN GOD'S PLAN

John the Baptist promised that Jesus would not just cleanse from sin but would renew and restore by giving God's Holy Spirit. On a number of occasions, Jesus referred to this gift of the Holy Spirit as "living water." In this miracle Jesus again demonstrated that he had come not merely to insist that people keep rules but to bring about real change.

AD 29 Jesus promises living water at the Feast of Tabernacles

AD 29 or 30 Jesus heals a blind man at the Pool of Siloam

Chalybeate (iron-rich) waters such as the springs in Tunbridge Wells, England, are said to renew energy and vitality.

Thermal springs such as Deildartunguhver in Iceland are used to soothe body aches.

Near the end of his ministry, Jesus told a story about a king who prepared a great banquet in honor of his son's wedding. He invited the people one would expect to find at a royal gala, yet they all refused to come. In response, the king

INVITING THE

Where it happened...
The setting of this parable is a fictitious kingdom

Many mythologies have banquet stories that are very different!

In the Baltic pagan religion of Romuva, the feast celebrating the end of winter tells of a grass snake crawling on the banquet table to bring good luck for the coming year.

sent his servant to invite the least worthy members of society. One man managed to enter without the proper clothing. His speechlessness upon being caught indicated this was not an innocent oversight. He was tied up and ejected.

POOR

DAILY READING PLAN

July 25: Matthew 22:1-14; Luke 14:15-24
July 26: Luke 16:19-31
July 27: Luke 18:9-17

MAJOR THEMES

WE ARE NEVER TOO GOOD FOR GOD. This parable was meant to shock. The idea of someone refusing the invitation of a king was unheard of! To do so was positively treasonous. But Jesus was comparing such behavior to those who feel that they are good enough because of their own efforts.

WE ARE NEVER TOO BAD FOR GOD. The other side of the coin is that even the most depraved can accept forgiveness and renewal from God. The picture of beggars at a palace is encouraging to all who recognize that we fall short of the holiness God demands.

WE ARE NEVER GOOD WITHOUT GOD. The implication of the story is that wedding garments were provided to the guests. To get in without such a garment assumed subterfuge or that the partygoer decided to remove the garment that was provided. To this day people try to dictate their own terms to God. To do so is to refuse a righteousness God wants to give that is unattainable by our efforts alone.

ITS PART IN GOD'S PLAN

By the end of Jesus' ministry, the conflict between the self-righteous religious establishment and Jesus had reached a boiling point. After three years, the fact that Jesus was sent from God could not be denied. Yet the self-righteous refused to humble themselves. They still believed they were worthy of God's approval, superior to the common and corrupt general population.

AD 29 or 30 Jesus tells the Parable of the Wedding Banquet

The New Fire Feast of the Aztecs required every household to destroy all cooking utensils, quench household fires, and relight them from the flames of a human sacrifice!

The feasts of the Greek god Dionysus were unrestrained celebrations of drunkenness and sensuality.

An expert in the Law of Moses asked Jesus how to please God and thereby gain eternal life. Jesus turned the question back on him. The man answered that the core values of the Law were loving God and loving one's neighbor, and Jesus agreed. When the expert asked Jesus who qualified to be a neighbor, Jesus told this story.

GOOD SAMARITAN

MAJOR THEMES

GOD'S DESIRE FOR OUR LIVES IS SIMPLE. The experts in Jewish Law read volume after volume of God's Law, the words of the prophets, and commentary about both. But they all could be summed up in two commands: 1) Love God. 2) Love people. But how does one show love to God? And which people are we obligated to love?

RULES THAT THWART COMPASSION ARE NOT GODLY. Jesus implied that two men were on their way to serve God in the temple at Jerusalem. The expert in the Law, to whom Jesus was speaking, knew why the priest and Levite would avoid the injured man. If he died in their care, they would be touching a dead body, making them ceremonially unfit to perform their ritualistic duties. Is God really pleased with worship that comes at the expense of meeting human needs?

HATRED POISONS OUR LIVES. The expert in the Law would have despised a Samaritan as much as he would have admired a priest or a Levite. But the Samaritan was not motivated by ritual or by racial prejudice. He did not stop to consider whether or not the injured man would repay him or, if the roles were reversed, would have done the same for him. Love for a neighbor may even include love for an enemy!

ITS PART IN GOD'S PLAN

Because Jesus was not a formally trained rabbi, Jewish leaders hoped to embarrass him by asking questions that scholars debated at length. But to their dismay—and to the delight of the common people—Jesus turned the tables on them with disarming simplicity.

AD **29** Jesus tells the Parable of the Good Samaritan

The Parable of the Good Samaritan still captures our imagination today:

Many U. S. states have Good Samaritan laws that protect someone from being sued who tries to help a stranger.

DAILY READING PLAN

July 28: Luke 10:25-37
July 29: Matthew 22:34-40
July 30: John 7:25-44

Where it happened...
The setting of this parable is
the road between Jerusalem
and Jericho

AD **30** Jesus teaches
about the Greatest
Commandment

"Good Samaritan" is used
as a name for hospitals and
medical centers throughout
the country.

OFFICIAL MEMBER
Good Sam
Club

The Good Sam Club began in 1966 when a group
of recreational vehicle owners put Good Samaritan
bumper stickers on their RVs so fellow members
would know they could get help on the road.

Upon hearing the news that Herod had executed John the Baptist, Jesus withdrew to a remote area. But crowds followed. Jesus spent the day teaching them and healing the sick. At nightfall, Jesus gathered the crowd of five

FEEDING FIVE

When it happened...
AD 29

Where it happened...
A remote place by the Sea of Galilee

DAILY READING PLAN
July 31: Matthew 14:1-21; Mark 6:14-44
August 1: John 6:1-15, 25-59
August 2: Matthew 15:29-39

AD **29**
Herod executes
John the Baptist

thousand men and an unspecified number of women and children and fed them with only two fish and five small loaves of bread. Remarkably, everyone had enough to eat, and twelve baskets of leftovers remained.

THOUSAND

MAJOR THEMES

JESUS CARES ABOUT OUR EMOTIONAL PAIN. John the Baptist was loved by the ordinary people of the day. The news of his execution would have been devastating to many. Jesus welcomed the crowd and comforted them with his words and healing miracles. Although the loss of John would have been painful for Jesus, he saw the emotional distress of the crowd and eased their spirits.

JESUS CARES ABOUT PHYSICAL NEEDS. Some religions teach that the needs of the body are somehow evil and must be denied. Jesus did not make such a distinction. He healed physical infirmities as well as spiritual ones. His words were a spiritual feast, to be sure, but Jesus also recognized the necessity of taming a growling stomach.

JESUS STAYS WITH US. The fact that thousands could be sated with a lunch barely enough for one was remarkable. But there were also leftovers! The leftovers were put into twelve small baskets, the type that one might use to carry food for a journey. Since there were twelve baskets and twelve disciples, it is likely that each disciple carried one with him as he continued to travel with Jesus. What a reminder of Jesus' continual provision!

ITS PART IN GOD'S PLAN

At the time of Moses, God fed his people with bread from Heaven. This miracle of Jesus was enough to convince the crowds that Jesus was the promised prophet, like Moses, who would lead God's eternal kingdom. But they had yet to learn that they needed a Messiah who would be able to give them much more than their next meal.

AD **29**
Jesus feeds 5,000

AD **29**
Jesus calls himself
the bread of life

AD **29**
Jesus feeds 4,000

Near the end of Jesus' ministry, opposition from the Jewish leaders became increasingly hostile. Contrasting himself to the authoritarian religious leaders, Jesus characterized himself as a humble shepherd who cared for his flock, even if it meant putting his life on the line for them.

THE GOOD

ITS PART IN GOD'S PLAN

The image of a shepherd would have elicited memories of Israel's greatest king, David. Unlike the Jewish leaders who threatened to remove dissenters from the community, Jesus spoke of having an even larger flock than the Jewish nation. In contrast to those who would try to retain their power at all cost, Jesus spoke frankly of giving his life for his subjects.

593–571 BC The prophet Ezekiel warns of the danger of false shepherds in Israel

The image of the shepherd is still seen in our culture:

"Shepherding" is a tactic in Australian-rules football that prevents an opposing player from taking possession of the ball.

SHEPHERD

MAJOR THEMES

NOT EVERY LEADER IS A SHEPHERD. One does not need to understand, know, or even care about his subjects to be a tyrant. But a shepherd is a different matter. A shepherd would lead a flock to a place of nourishment. A shepherd would always be aware of possible threats to the flock. A shepherd would be able to individually identify any one sheep in a hundred, know the temperament of that sheep, and even have a distinct name for it! Tyrants see their subjects as interchangeable parts meant to serve them. Not so with shepherds.

GOD WANTS FOLLOWERS FROM ALL NATIONS. While many Jews still had the idea that the coming Messiah would throw off Roman rule and restore Israel as a nation once more, God had a better idea. Over the centuries the Jews came to view all other nations as the beasts who threatened to devour the flock of God. Jesus taught that those who are far from God are not wolves, but future sheep to be brought into his flock.

AN ETERNAL SHEPHERD BRINGS SECURITY TO HIS FLOCK. A shepherd would insert himself between the enemy and the flock in his care. If the shepherd could frighten away or kill the intruding beasts, the flock was safe. But if the shepherd were killed, the flock was doomed. Jesus, however, hinted that his life could not be taken from him. Having an invulnerable shepherd makes for a very safe flock!

DAILY READING PLAN

August 3: Ezekiel 34
August 4: Matthew 18:12-14; Luke 15:1-7
August 5: John 10:1-16

AD 29 or 30
Jesus identifies himself
as the Good Shepherd

The shepherding movement emerged as a style of Christian discipleship in charismatic churches in the 1970s.

On the popular television program *Lost*, the leader and protector of a band of people marooned on a strange island is named Jack Shephard. His father was Christian Shephard.

At the beginning of his ministry, Jesus attended a wedding feast with his disciples and his mother. After his mother, Mary, told him that the host was out of wine, Jesus ordered the servants to do two things. First, they were to fill the

WATER AND

ITS PART IN GOD'S PLAN

Jesus often referred to water both in his teaching and by his miracles. He offered the woman at the well living water that would become a flowing spring within. He offered the disabled man at Bethesda Pool the complete healing that the therapeutic waters could not give. Jesus even walked on the surface of the water and commanded the waves of the sea! Jesus was more than just another prophet who taught rules about moral purity. He could give the renewing Spirit of God.

When it happened...
AD 26 or 27

Where it happened...
Cana in Galilee

Wine in ancient China was made from rice, possibly mixed with grapes. Very early archaeological finds in Iran attest to wine-making from grapes. And evidence of ancient wine-making in Greece has been found as well.

ceremonial washing jars to the brim. Then they were to draw water and present it to the host, who proclaimed that it was the finest wine. This miracle revealed who Jesus was, and his disciples placed their faith in him.

WINE

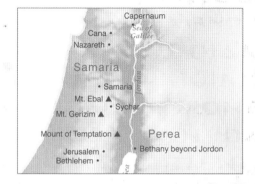

DAILY READING PLAN
August 6: John 2:1-11
August 7: Mark 7:1-5
August 8: Ephesians 5:8-20

MAJOR THEMES

GOD PROVIDES SUFFICIENT EVIDENCE TO INSPIRE TRUST. Changing one's belief system is not a decision made quickly. Jesus' first disciples followed John the Baptist, who told them who Jesus was. But it was not until after this miracle that they got it. Jesus was the one who would baptize with the Holy Spirit.

THE JEWISH LAW CANNOT COMPLETELY RESTORE HUMANKIND TO GOD. The stone jars were used for ceremonial washing. They reminded the Jews of the need to be cleansed to be right with God. The number six (the number of these jars) often signified to the ancient mind a lack of completion. Could Jesus have been showing that even filled to the brim, the cleansing that came from Jewish ritual was incomplete?

JESUS OFFERS RENEWAL FROM WITHIN. On the Day of Pentecost, Peter would say that the believers were not drunk but filled with the Holy Spirit. And Paul later told the Ephesians to be filled with the Spirit, not with alcohol. Alcoholic spirits enter the bloodstream and are delivered to every part of the body. On the day of this miracle, Jesus wanted people to grasp that the Holy Spirit would do more than just cleanse from sin; he would enter a person and be able to affect every thought and action. The contrast between water and wine clearly illustrated what John had said about Jesus!

AD **26 or 27**
Jesus turns water
into wine

AD **26 or 27**
Jesus promises the Samaritan
woman living water

In the early days of Jesus' ministry, Nicodemus, a member of the Sanhedrin (the Jewish ruling council), came to him at night. Jesus spoke to him frankly about the need to be born again. Jesus spoke of this second birth having two

JESUS AND

When it happened...
AD 26 or 27

Where it happened...
Jerusalem

ITS PART IN GOD'S PLAN

Jesus confirmed to Nicodemus that he agreed with John's assessment that all human beings—Jews and non-Jews—must admit and repudiate their rebellion against God. Jesus further identified himself as the Son of God who had come to save the world. Jesus would renew human beings with the Holy Spirit after paying for their rebellion with his own life. Sometime in the following three years, Nicodemus came to believe that message.

c. 1445 BC God commanded Moses to choose 70 elders from among the people

c. 75 BC The council of the elders renamed the Sanhedrin

AD 26 or 27 Nicodemus, a member of the Sanhedrin, comes to Jesus at night

elements—being born of the water and being born of the Spirit. This message seems to reiterate that of John the Baptist—the necessity of cleansing from sin and of being renewed by the Holy Spirit.

NICODEMUS

MAJOR THEMES

JESUS QUICKLY ATTRACTED ATTENTION FROM HIGH PLACES. One may question the reason for Nicodemus's visit. Was he personally curious and visited at night so his search for truth would remain secret? Or was he sent from the ruling council to investigate this new teacher, avoiding confrontations with the crowds, which had occurred when leaders came to investigate John earlier? Either way, a visit from a member of the ruling council of the Jews showed that, from the beginning, Jesus could not be ignored!

GOD ALLOWS THE ULTIMATE DO-OVER. Humankind had made a mess of things. God could have easily turned away and allowed us to live and die in the misery we created. But the message of Jesus was that God would make a way for human beings to be reborn.

OUR REBIRTH COMES AT JESUS' EXPENSE. This second chance has a huge price tag. The payment for treason is death. In talking with Nicodemus, Jesus referred to the account of the rebellious Israelites in the wilderness with Moses centuries earlier. Motivated by God's love for humankind, Jesus would provide the once-and-for-all antidote to the serpent's poison—with his own life.

DAILY READING PLAN

August 9: John 3:1-21; 12:32, 33; 19:38, 39
August 10: Romans 5:6-11; 6:1-10
August 11: Philippians 2:5-11

AD **30** Nicodemus and Joseph of Arimathea make arrangements for Jesus' burial

AD **358** Sanhedrin disbanded

AD **1806** Napoleon Bonaparte attempts to revive the Sanhedrin by appointing his Great Sanhedrin

When crowds gathered on a mountainside in Galilee, Jesus gave one of his longest recorded sermons—a sort of inaugural address of the kingdom of God. In the Sermon on the Mount, Jesus defined the lifestyle of those who would be a part of his eternal kingdom.

SERMON ON

When it happened...
AD 28

Where it happened...
Galilee

What a sermon! All of this and more is in the Sermon on the Mount:
The Beatitudes (Blessed are . . .)
The command to be "the salt of the earth" and "the light of the world"
The Lord's Prayer
The Golden Rule

DAILY READING PLAN

August 12: Matthew 5   **August 14:** Matthew 7
August 13: Matthew 6   **August 15:** Luke 6:17-49

THE MOUNT

MAJOR THEMES

FOLLOWERS OF JESUS HAVE A NEW STANDARD OF HAPPINESS. The sermon begins with sayings commonly called the Beatitudes, prescriptions for happiness. These sayings are counterintuitive—they speak of finding happiness in mourning, hunger, and persecution! But Jesus was not teaching that we should get pleasure from pain. Rather, he was saying we can endure pain, knowing that it is not the final state of those who trust him.

FOLLOWERS OF JESUS HAVE A NEW STANDARD OF MORALITY. The Pharisees were known for their rigorous law keeping. The scribes were revered for their study of the Law of Moses. But members of the kingdom of the new covenant would have an even higher standard of righteousness! How could that possibly be? Kingdom citizens would learn that regeneration by the Holy Spirit could produce virtue that human effort cannot.

FOLLOWERS OF JESUS HAVE A LEADER WITH ABSOLUTE AUTHORITY. In the four centuries following the prophet Malachi, there was no one to speak a direct word from God. The teachers of the Law discussed and commented on the words of Moses and the prophets, but crowds recognized Jesus' sermon as something qualitatively different. He spoke with real authority, an authority that would be foundational to a new kind of life.

ITS PART IN GOD'S PLAN

Moses brought the stipulations of the old covenant from Mt. Sinai. Jesus spoke the terms of the new covenant on this mountainside in Galilee. But the new covenant would not contradict the old covenant. Rather, Jesus would create a way in which the standards of the Law of Moses could be met and internalized in those who trusted in him.

AD **28** Jesus preaches the Sermon on the Mount

Throughout his ministry, Jesus almost seemed to go out of his way to irritate legalists! A regular target was ritual Sabbath observance. When Jesus did not stop his disciples from picking grain and feeding themselves on the Sabbath, some Pharisees cited this as a violation of their traditional observance of the day.

When it happened...	Where it happened...
AD 28	Galilee

MAJOR THEMES

RULES ARE FOR OUR GOOD, NOT OUR GOODNESS. The Sabbath Day was instituted by God for a number of reasons, not the least of which was that people be refreshed. Jesus chided the Pharisees for acting as if human beings were created so they could please God by keeping arbitrary rules. The truth is that God's rules, including the Sabbath, were given with our best interest in mind.

LEGALISM CAN TURN TO APATHY. Legalists witness a man walking who had been disabled for decades. They witness a man blind from birth who now has perfect vision. They witness other physical disabilities shrink in an instant. But all they see are Sabbath breakers! Instead of rejoicing with people freed from suffering, legalists look for ways to place them back in bondage.

LEGALISM CAN TURN TO HATRED. Jesus did not just disagree with the Pharisees and leave it at that. He performed miracles that were undeniable and that demonstrated his authority to reverse their interpretation of the rules of God. But these miracles that should have brought about obedience hardened the Pharisees' opposition to Jesus. When they saw they could not win an argument, their thoughts turned to violence.

DAILY READING PLAN

August 16: Luke 4:31-37

August 17: Matthew 12:1-8; Mark 2:23-28; Luke 6:1-5

August 18: Matthew 12:9-14; Mark 3:1-6; Luke 6:6-11

August 19: Luke 13:10-17; 14:1-6

August 20: John 5:8-18; 7:21-24

August 21: John 9:13-34

AD 26 Jesus casts out a demon on the Sabbath

AD 28 Jesus' disciples pick grain on the Sabbath

AD 28 Jesus heals a man with a shriveled hand on the Sabbath

SABBATH
CONTROVERSIES

ITS PART IN GOD'S PLAN

Keeping a day dedicated to rest and worship was modeled in creation and was commanded in the Law of Moses. But in Jesus' day, ritualistic Sabbath keeping had become a sort of spiritual litmus test. Jesus challenged the Pharisees' mistaken idea that keeping the Sabbath was to be observed at the expense of people who were suffering. He put human need above ritualistic observance—and doing so raised the ire of the religious leaders.

c. AD 29 Jesus heals the man at Bethesda Pool on the Sabbath

c. AD 29 Jesus heals a crippled woman on the Sabbath

AD 29 Jesus heals a blind man on the Sabbath

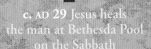

SEE THE HOLY LAND

Even after about two and a half years with Jesus, the disciples still struggled to understand exactly who he was and how he fit into God's plan. When Jesus frankly asked the twelve who they thought he was, Peter quickly said that he was

THE TRANSFIGURATION

MAJOR THEMES

JESUS IS MORE THAN A PROPHET. On the mountain Jesus displayed a radiance that had been associated with the glory of God throughout the Old Testament. With him appeared the two men who embodied the Law and the prophets—Moses and Elijah. While many speculated that Jesus was just another prophet, his glorified appearance, as he stood before two of the greatest of God's servants from the past, showed him to be much more.

JESUS IS MASTER OF LIFE AND DEATH. Jews of that day thought the Messiah would be a king. He would defeat his enemies and assume the throne of David. The idea of a Messiah who would be executed was disturbing to Peter, even though Jesus promised to be raised from the dead. Seeing Jesus literally shining like the sun helped Peter and the others understand that death was no match for their master.

JESUS IS GOD'S FINAL WORD. If the appearance of a man illuminated with the light of God and standing with two long-dead heroes wasn't enough, there was more! A cloud, reminding them of the presence of God leading Israel to the promised land, enveloped them. Then the voice of God commanded them to listen to Jesus alone. Moses and Elijah were history; Jesus was eternity!

DAILY READING PLAN

August 22: Matthew 16:13-28

August 23: Matthew 17:1-13

August 24: 2 Peter 1:12-21; John 1:14; 1 John 1:1-4

August 25: Hebrews 1:1-3; 3:1-6

AD **29**
Peter avers that he believes
Jesus is the Messiah

the Messiah. But Peter balked at the idea of the Christ suffering and dying. Jesus took Peter, James, and John to the top of a mountain where the mystery of his identity was revealed.

ITS PART IN GOD'S PLAN

Jesus did not come to make Israel better; Jesus came to make God's plan complete. Even Jesus' closest disciples saw him as a new teacher who would bring back the glory days of the past. This extraordinary revelation on the mountain indicated that Jesus had not come to restore the nation of Israel but to bring all humankind to him forever.

When it happened...
AD 29

Where it happened...
Thought to have occurred at Mt. Hermon

AD 29
Jesus' divine nature is clearly revealed to three disciples

c. AD 64 Peter refers to the transfiguration when writing to a new generation of believers

As Jesus and his disciples were heading toward Jerusalem at the end of his ministry, a prominent young man approached them. The young man asked what he must do to earn eternal life. Jesus' reply discouraged him and shocked the disciples. Jesus explained further with a parable that some religious people to this day consider scandalous!

When it happened...
AD 30

Where it happened...
On the way to Jerusalem

THE RICH

AD **30** Jesus explains that we must come to him like little children

Some of the richest people in history:

Croesus—The name of this king of Lydia in the 6th century BC is a synonym for a wealthy man. Someone with great wealth may be referred to as "richer than Croesus."

YOUNG RULER

THERE ARE NO GOOD PEOPLE. The young man seemed to have it all. He was wealthy, powerful, and by community standards, morally upright. But all people are rebels against God. Asking what good deeds will bring one to God is like a traitor asking how many times he needs to wave the flag in order to be repatriated.

THERE IS NO EASY WAY TO GOD. The road between humankind and God washed out with Adam and Eve. The gulf is so great that no human effort can bridge it. But while there is no easy way to God, Jesus has made *the way* to God. It is based on his work, not ours.

THERE IS ONE THING WE CAN GIVE TO GOD. And that is our unconditional surrender! Attempts to win God's favor or impress him with our wealth or power are not acts of piety. Trying to be good enough for God is simply another way to rebel against him. It is saying that our transgressions against him are minor and our righteousness is relatively great.

MAJOR THEMES

ITS PART IN GOD'S PLAN

Jesus followed this encounter with a story about workers in a vineyard. Some worked all day, and some worked fractions of a day. Nevertheless, all were paid for a full day's work! The idea that all that we do for God somehow earns us a reward is as ingrained in religious thinking today as it was in the days of the first disciples. And it is just as wrong now as it was then.

AD **30**
Jesus speaks to a rich young ruler

AD **30**
Jesus tells the Parable of the Workers in the Vineyard

Mansa Musa—This 14th century west African king traveled with an entourage of 60,000 men, 500 of whom marched before him dressed in silken robes and holding golden staffs.

The Medicis—Members of this 15th century Italian banking family held prominent positions of power in the country and in the Catholic Church.

Jewish leaders opposed Jesus, but all opposed him for different reasons. During the last week of Jesus' life, leaders of different Jewish denominations of the day peppered Jesus with trick questions designed to embarrass him before his followers. Jesus' answers, however, only succeeded in elevating his status as a great teacher!

TRICK

ITS PART IN GOD'S PLAN

To this day, many would like to attack Jesus and his followers as being politically incorrect, superstitious, or simpleminded. Yet Jesus' answers to his opponents two thousand years ago are as relevant today as they were then!

AD **30** Pharisees and Herodians question Jesus about paying taxes to Caesar

AD **30** Sadducees question Jesus about the nature of the afterlife

AD **30** Pharisees question Jesus about the priority of commandments

Roman coins:
Denarius—silver coin, the daily wage of an average working man

Aureus—gold coin, worth 25 denarii

QUESTIONS

DAILY READING PLAN
August 29: Matthew 22:15-40
August 30: Romans 13:1-7
August 31: Matthew 23

MAJOR THEMES

POLITICAL ACTIVISTS TRIED TO TRAP JESUS. The Herodians were Jews who sought to appease the Roman government. They reasoned that if Jesus approved of paying taxes to Rome, he would anger the common people. If he did not approve, Rome would consider him an insurrectionist. But by using a simple Roman coin, Jesus answered that it was possible to support Caesar while maintaining an overriding loyalty to God.

RELIGIOUS SKEPTICS TRIED TO RIDICULE JESUS. The Sadducees disbelieved in life after death and angelic beings, so they created a complicated straw-man argument about polygamy in the afterlife! Jesus pointed out that by denying supernatural realities, they denied the Scriptures and the power of God. Their "enlightened Judaism" was not Judaism at all.

SCHOLARS TRIED TO DISCREDIT JESUS. The Pharisees and scribes had spent centuries analyzing and commenting on the Law of Moses, to the point that it had become a complicated intellectual exercise. They tried to show that Jesus was ignorant of the scholarly arguments concerning which laws were the greatest. Jesus discredited them by showing that their "deep" question had a surprisingly simple answer!

Sestertius— bronze coin, worth one-quarter of a denarius

Dupondius— bronze coin, worth one-fifth of a denarius

As— copper coin, worth one-tenth of a denarius

Jesus had performed an undeniable miracle just outside Jerusalem—he raised a man back to life who had been dead for four days. Given this notoriety, avoiding the crowd gathered in Jerusalem for the Passover was impossible. Jesus knew he would be welcomed as the king of the Jews, but he chose to ride into town on an unlikely animal.

TRIUMPHAL

ITS PART IN GOD'S PLAN

Jesus' last week before the crucifixion began with his being welcomed as a conquering king. By the end of that week, many in that same crowd would be calling for his execution. But both events were necessary as God's plan to save the world reached its climax.

AD **30**
Jesus raises Lazarus
from the grave

There are three festivals during which the Jews in Jesus' day would travel to Jerusalem:

Passover—celebrated in March or April, recalls Moses leading the Israelites out of Egypt.

When it happened...
AD 30

Where it happened...
Jerusalem

ENTRY

MAJOR THEMES

JESUS CAME AS A HUMBLE KING. A conquering king would typically ride into a town on a strong white horse. Jesus chose to enter Jerusalem on a servant's mount, a young donkey. Shortly before this event, two of Jesus' disciples lobbied him for high positions in the nation he would lead. Jesus responded that he had not come to be served but to serve. Perhaps it was those same two disciples that Jesus sent for the colt.

JESUS CAME AS THE PROMISED KING. The prophet Zechariah had promised that the Messiah would enter Jerusalem on the foal of a donkey. That same prophet spoke of the celebration of Tabernacles, the Jewish harvest festival, at his coming. Although the feast about to be celebrated in Jerusalem was Passover, the crowd responded to Jesus as though it were Tabernacles. Waving palm branches and reciting Psalm 118:26 to welcome the one who comes in the name of the Lord are a part of the Tabernacles celebration to this day. The crowd clearly recognized who Jesus was.

JESUS CAME AS THE WHOLE WORLD'S KING. Some Pharisees were so offended by the crowd's reaction that they told Jesus to silence the crowd. He responded that if every human voice were stilled, inanimate rocks would gain a voice and welcome him! The Messiah would do more than save the Jews—he would change the entire world!

DAILY READING PLAN
September 1: Leviticus 23:40; Psalm 118:26; Zechariah 9:9-13; 14:16
September 2: Matthew 21:1-11; Mark 11:1-11
September 3: Luke 19:28-44
September 4: John 12:12-19

AD 30
Jesus tells his disciples that he came to be the ransom for many

AD 30
Jesus enters Jerusalem on a donkey's colt

Feast of Weeks (Pentecost)—observed in May or June to celebrate spring harvest and the giving of the 10 Commandments to Moses.

Tabernacles—a thanksgiving and harvest festival celebrated in September or October, recalls the Israelites in the wilderness on the way to the promised land.

Some time after his arrival in Jerusalem, Jesus entered the temple area, where he found men selling sacrificial animals to those coming to celebrate Passover. He overturned their tables and drove them out. The leaders were indignant and plotted to kill Jesus. The crowds of common people, however, continued to praise and follow him.

CLEANSING THE

When it happened...
AD 30

Where it happened...
Jerusalem

959 BC First temple dedicated during the rule of Solomon

536 BC Foundation of the second temple laid by returning exiles

HOYASMEG

c. 20 BC—Renovation of temple by Herod the Great begins

TEMPLE

MAJOR THEMES

SOME THINGS BEAR REPEATING. Jesus' public ministry can be seen as being bracketed with two occasions of cleansing the temple. On the first Passover he celebrated with his disciples, he fashioned a whip and drove the merchants from the temple court. On this fourth Passover, three years later, he acted in a similar fashion.

RELIGION CAN BE USED TO ENSLAVE RATHER THAN FREE. The Law of Moses required that sacrifices offered to God be of the highest quality. Offering something one does not want is not sacrifice but disposal! Apparently, some stationed in the temple court to approve sacrifices actually rejected acceptable animals in order to sell worshipers their own merchandise at a profit. Such abuse of people in the name of piety angered Jesus.

THE TEMPLE POINTED TO SOMETHING GREATER. During the first cleansing of the temple, the leaders asked Jesus to show some sign that he was authorized to take such action. Jesus told them to tear down the temple and he would raise it in three days. Of course, this met with ridicule. But three years later, what Jesus had spoken of would happen. These leaders would try to destroy the structure that contained the true presence of God—Jesus himself.

ITS PART IN GOD'S PLAN

The temple (and the tabernacle before it) was crucial to following the Law of Moses. But four decades after this time, the Roman army would destroy the temple. It has not been rebuilt since. A greater vessel that housed the presence of God was then present—Jesus. And a "vessel" that would continue to house the presence of God was about to be built—the church; that is, all believers worldwide.

AD 26
First cleansing
of the temple

AD 30
Second cleansing
of the temple

AD 70—The Roman
army led by Titus
destroys the temple

Jesus made preparations with his disciples to eat the Passover meal in the upper room of a house in Jerusalem. During that meal, Jesus imbued it with new meaning and spoke frankly to his disciples about their relationship with him and with one another. To this day the church celebrates this meal with the understanding that Jesus fulfilled it.

THE LAST SUPPER

When it happened...
AD 30

Where it happened...
Jerusalem

MAJOR THEMES

A NEW PASSOVER IS HERE. On the first Passover, the Jews prepared to flee Egypt. They did not have time for bread to rise, so they made it without yeast. They sacrificed a lamb and smeared its blood on the doorposts of their houses, trusting that the plague of death sent to Egypt would pass over them. But all those events had a deeper meaning.

JESUS LOVES US TO DEATH! In the Lord's Supper, Jesus himself is identified as the Passover lamb who was sacrificed so his people would escape death. Jesus took the familiar elements of the Passover celebration and told his disciples how they testified to what he was about to suffer to pay the price for the world's rebellion. The Lord's Supper stands as a continual reminder that a terrible price was paid because of God's love for us.

THERE IS ONE CHURCH. The Passover, in many ways, was a signature celebration of Judaism. But during the Last Supper, Jesus told of the signature mark of his church—a deep love for one another. When the church celebrates the Lord's Supper, we do so in conjunction with believers all around the world, pledging our love for and unity with them because of our mutual thanksgiving to Jesus.

ITS PART IN GOD'S PLAN

We call it the Lord's Supper, Communion (sharing together), and the Eucharist (gratitude). This celebration is all the above. Through the centuries that last Passover meal of Jesus and his disciples has been reenacted countless times with followers of Jesus in every part of the world.

AD 30 Jesus celebrates the Passover meal with his disciples

AD 55 Paul corrects the church in Corinth concerning their lack of unity in celebrating the Lord's Supper

Sometime between AD 100–150
An early nonbiblical Christian book, the Didache, gives instructions concerning the Lord's Supper

c. AD 150 An early defender of Christianity, Justin Martyr, speaks of bringing the elements of the Lord's Supper to those who were absent from a worship service

c. AD 1517–1563 Differences between Protestant and Catholic understanding of the nature of the Lord's Supper become clearly defined

After sharing the Passover meal with his disciples, Jesus went to Gethsemane. Judas had already gone to lead the soldiers to arrest Jesus there. In the meantime, as Jesus prayed, he endured such distress that his sweat was like drops of blood. He did not want to die, but he would not succumb to the temptation of placing his own agenda before God's agenda.

IN THE GARDEN

MAJOR THEMES

SATAN IS AN OPPORTUNIST. Before Jesus even began his ministry, Satan tried to derail it. We are told that since Jesus resisted him, Satan looked for another opportunity. Those moments before Jesus' arrest were an opportune time. Jesus was overwhelmed by the sacrifice he was called to make. He went to his Father in prayer in Gethsemane, just as he had three years earlier in the wilderness.

WE ARE NOT AS STRONG AS WE THINK. In the upper room Peter promised he would not leave Jesus and would defend him to the end. But when Jesus asked the disciples to pray in the garden, they could not even stay awake. Later, all of them, including Peter, fled as Jesus was arrested. Even when we desire to do right, our physical limitations and our fears weaken our best efforts.

GOD'S WILL TRUMPS ALL ELSE. Adam and Eve put their desires first. Jesus (who is called the "last Adam") prayed that God's will be done. Jesus, being fully human, would experience the pain of abandonment and execution, and certainly desired to avoid feeling God's wrath for the sins of the world. Adam wanted to be like God; Jesus allowed himself to take the penalty for all humans. This is the contrast between the Garden of Eden and the Garden of Gethsemane.

ITS PART IN GOD'S PLAN

Jesus' final response to God's plans for him was given in the Garden of Gethsemane. He knew his arrest was imminent. But instead of running from it, he made the anguished decision to take the cup of God's wrath as his own. The events of the next day were determined by Jesus' obedience the night before.

AD 30 Judas agrees to betray Jesus for 30 silver pieces

AD 30 Judas leaves the Passover celebration to alert the soldiers who would arrest Jesus

Judas is considered one of the biggest traitors in history. Here are a few others:

c. 415 BC Alcibiades, an Athenian, joined with Sparta, then left the Spartans and rejoined the Athenians.

AD 1605 Guy Fawkes, a British citizen, tried to blow up the English king and Parliament while they were in session.

DAILY READING PLAN

September 14: Matthew 26:36-56   **September 16:** Luke 22:39-65
September 15: Mark 14:32-52   **September 17:** John 17:1–18:11

OF GETHSEMANE

When it happened...
AD 30

Where it happened...
Garden of Gethsemane
outside Jerusalem

AD 30 Jesus prays in the Garden of Gethsemane. Soldiers arrest Jesus, and his disciples flee.

AD 1780 Benedict Arnold, an American general, took command of West Point in order to surrender it to the British.

AD 1792 Magdalena Rudenschöld, a Swedish noblewoman, committed treason against the king to win back her lover.

Throughout the night, the Jewish leaders put Jesus on trial and attempted to get Roman leaders to condemn him to death. That next day, Jesus was mocked, scourged, forced to carry the tool for his own execution, and nailed to that cross where he slowly and painfully suffocated. But this horrible event was not without purpose.

THE CRUCIFIXION

MAJOR THEMES

THE CRUCIFIXION WAS SACRIFICE, NOT MARTYRDOM. A martyr is someone fighting for a cause who happens to get caught (or gives himself up) and dies. A martyr could be anybody. Not so in this case. Only the perfect Lamb of God could be a Passover sacrifice. Jesus was not a victim. Jesus' life was not given to raise awareness but to literally raise the dead!

THE CRUCIFIXION WAS THE CONCLUSION, NOT THE END. With Jesus' last words he proclaimed that it was finished. *What* was finished? Not his life. That would be evident three days later! Rather, his mission was complete. He had given his life to pay for the debt of Adam.

THE CRUCIFIXION WAS PLANNED, NOT TRAGIC. On the cross, Jesus began to call out the words of Psalm 22 in the language of his fellow Jews. This song, written by King David one thousand years earlier, described the crucifixion in detail. Those who recognized the source of those words would only have to look around to see the predictions coming true: people mocking and insulting, Jesus' pierced hands and feet, and people casting lots for his clothing.

ITS PART IN GOD'S PLAN

It is hard to imagine a more horrible sight than a Roman crucifixion, especially when a man innocent of even the smallest wrongdoing suffered it. But this was not the end. The crucifixion paid for the sins of humanity. And the events of the next days would pave the way for the rebirth of humanity.

AD 30
Jesus put on trial

Other crucifixions in history:

c. 484 BC Greek writer Herodotus gave details of the crucifixion of a traitor.

DALL'ORTO

c. 71 BC About 6,000 slaves, led to revolt by Spartacus, were crucified along the 125-mile road between Capua and Rome, as a warning to any other would-be rebels.

When it happened...
AD 30

Where it happened...
Golgotha (meaning "skull")
outside Jerusalem

DAILY READING PLAN

September 18: Psalm 22
September 19: Matthew 27:32-44
September 20: Mark 15:21-32
September 21: Luke 23:26-43
September 22: John 19:16-27

AD **30**
Jesus mocked and scourged
by Roman soldiers

AD **30**
Jesus crucified

AD **1597** 26 Christians
were nailed to crosses in
Nagasaki, Japan.

AD **1915** Germans
were reported to have
crucified a Canadian
prisoner during WWI.

The Crucifixion · 167

Jesus was crucified at 9:00 AM. At noon the skies became dark until he died three hours later. At his death remarkable events happened, signifying a great change between the relationship of humanity and God. Two secret disciples of high rank took down Jesus' body from the cross and buried him in a tomb cut out of a rocky hillside.

FROM THE CROSS

ITS PART IN GOD'S PLAN

Jesus had to die so that the sins of the world could be forgiven. But even Jesus' lifeless body told that there was more to the story. John the Baptist and Jesus taught of the two parts of salvation—forgiveness and renewal. They talked about water and the Spirit, water and wine, water and living water. When the soldiers pierced Jesus' side, that theme was repeated when they saw water and blood. Cleansing had occurred. Renewal was next!

When it happened...
AD 30

Where it happened...
Jerusalem

AD **30** The skies darken during Jesus' crucifixion

Burial practices around the world:

The Incans mummified prominent citizens, usually in a sitting position.

"Sky burial" is still the practice among the common people of Tibet. Corpses are dismembered and left on high places for birds of prey. Bodies of other citizens are disposed of in different ways: children at sea, car accident victims by fire, and high-ranking people (like lamas) in tombs.

TO THE TOMB

MAJOR THEMES

THE PRIEST WAS THE SACRIFICE. Crucifixion was a slow process. Sometimes executioners would build smoky fires to help suffocate the victim or break a victim's legs to speed death. But in Jesus' case the executioners found that he had died quickly. The reason was that Jesus was not the victim of an execution. He was a priest who offered himself as a sacrifice. His life was not taken; it was given.

JESUS' DEATH BROUGHT IMMEDIATE CHANGES. For the last three hours Jesus was on the cross, the skies were dark, even though it was midday. But at the death of Jesus, the sun shone again. What's more, the earth literally shook, and people once dead and buried came to life. Most significantly, the heavy curtain that blocked access to the most holy place in the temple was split from top to bottom. With the price of human rebellion paid, access to God was again possible.

JESUS HAS DISCIPLES IN UNLIKELY PLACES. The Jewish council had conspired to have Jesus crucified. But at least two council members had become disciples of Jesus. Nicodemus, who had once questioned Jesus about being born again, was one of them. Joseph of Arimathea, another, owned a new tomb and had Jesus buried there. They were not in the majority, but they would make a difference.

DAILY READING PLAN

September 23: Matthew 27:45-66; Mark 15:33-47

September 24: Luke 23:44-56; John 19:28-42

September 25: Hebrews 10:1-25

AD **30** Jesus dies and the earth shakes, tombs open, and the temple veil splits

AD **30** Jesus placed in a tomb owned by Joseph of Arimathea

The Beothuk natives of Newfoundland wrapped the bodies of the dead in birch bark and buried them in isolated locations.

The Apayao people of the Philippines often bury deceased persons under the kitchens of their homes.

Jesus was buried at dusk on Friday. Because the Sabbath began at that time, friends would not be able to complete the preservation of his body until Sunday morning. When the women who followed Jesus came to the tomb, they found Jesus' body gone and told his disciples.

ITS PART IN GOD'S PLAN

The resurrection is the linchpin of the Christian faith. This singular event holds together all the teachings of Jesus and his disciples. Because of its importance, one would think that God would find it necessary to demonstrate clearly that the resurrection in fact occurred. He did.

AD **30** Jesus rises from the dead on the third day

NASER SANTAPURAM

Jesus did not have something other religious leaders had—a body that stayed dead!

The Mosque of the Prophet (Al-Masjid al-Nabawi) in Medina is Islam's second most sacred site and stands above Muhammad's tomb.

Kushinagar, India, is a pilgrimage site for Buddhists. It was here that Buddha died and was cremated.

THE RESURRECTION

MAJOR THEMES

RESURRECTION THREATENS THE POWERFUL. The Jewish council bribed the guards to cover up Jesus' resurrection. The Sadducees taught that there was no life after death, so a confirmed resurrection undermined their authority. Both the Jewish and Roman leaders would have recognized a more frightening fact: people who believe they can survive death are impossible to oppress. Those in power did not want the story to get out.

RESURRECTION CONFUSES THE DOUBTFUL. Finding an empty tomb frightened and bewildered the women who came there. The immediate reaction of the apostles who heard those women's story was skepticism. Even upon finding the empty burial garments of Jesus, Peter wondered what had happened. In a world where everything dies, resurrection is not an easy concept to grasp.

RESURRECTION CONFIRMS WHAT WAS PREDICTED. The angel reminded the followers of Jesus that his resurrection should not have come as a surprise. After all, for his last months with them, Jesus had been consistently teaching that he would be executed and then raised in three days. It would take time for the disciples to work through those past predictions, but they would soon recall what was said and see the event clearly.

When it happened...
AD 30

Where it happened...
Jerusalem

Baha'u'llah, founder of the Baha'i Faith, died May 29, 1892. He was buried next to the Mansion at Bahji in Acre, Israel.

EVIL SALTINE

L. Ron Hubbard, science fiction author and founder of the Church of Scientology, died of a stroke on January 24, 1986, in Creston, California. His body was cremated.

After his resurrection, Jesus appeared to his followers a number of times and in a variety of places. He spoke to discouraged followers walking to the town of Emmaus. He ate a meal with the disciples on the seashore. He invited doubting Thomas to examine the wounds of his crucifixion. The resurrection was too important not to be confirmed over and over again.

PROOF OF LIFE

When it happened...
AD 30

Where it happened...
Jerusalem and the
surrounding areas,
Galilee

AD **30** Jesus appears
to the women near
his tomb

AD **30** Jesus appears to
two disciples on the
road to Emmaus

AD **30** Jesus appears to
most of his disciples
behind locked doors

MAJOR THEMES

MULTIPLE WITNESSES SAW THE RESURRECTED JESUS. Almost twenty-five years after the resurrection, the apostle Paul had an answer to those who doubted the resurrection—ask someone who was there! Jesus appeared many times after his resurrection and to as many as five hundred people at once. All those witnesses presented crucial testimony for the first decades of the church.

THE RESURRECTED JESUS WAS NOT A GHOST. The resurrection of Jesus was an empirical, physical one—not a mystical, spiritual one. After his resurrection, Jesus invited his disciples to examine the wounds of his crucifixion. He ate with them. He even went fishing with them. An important part of the disciples' message was not only that they saw and heard Jesus but also that they touched the resurrected Christ.

JESUS TOOK CARE OF UNFINISHED BUSINESS. On an earlier occasion Jesus had sent his disciples just to Israel. But after his death he gave a greater task—he would send them into the entire world. Peter, who had denied Jesus three times after promising undying loyalty hours before Jesus' arrest, needed to know Jesus' forgiveness. The resurrected Jesus made a point of having Peter reaffirm his love—the same number of times Peter had denied Jesus!

ITS PART IN GOD'S PLAN

The faith demanded by Jesus was not blind faith. The legitimacy of Christianity does not hinge on visions of a single person or subjective feelings of his disciples. Just as Jesus backed up his teaching with undeniable miracles, he demonstrated the truth of his resurrection with undeniable appearances.

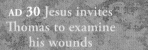

AD 30 Jesus invites Thomas to examine his wounds

AD 30 Jesus eats with his disciples on the shore of Galilee

AD 30 Jesus appears to a group of 500 at one time

For forty days after his resurrection, Jesus appeared to his followers time and time again. He did so to fully convince them that he was alive and also to allow his apostles to understand his teaching in light of his resurrection. Then Jesus

FORTY DAYS OF

DAILY READING PLAN

October 3: Matthew 28:18-20; Mark 16:15-20
October 4: Acts 1:1-5
October 5: Luke 24:50-53; Acts 1:6-11
October 6: Acts 1:12-26

AD **30** Jesus is crucified and rises from the dead during the Passover celebration

AD **30** Jesus teaches his disciples for 40 days following the resurrection

Other important 40-day periods in Scripture:

God prepared a "clean" world with the 40-day rain of Noah's flood.

Moses spent 40 days on Mt. Sinai receiving the commandments of God.

promised that the Holy Spirit would come upon them in Jerusalem to equip them for worldwide ministry. And as he ascended into Heaven, angels promised that he would return in the future.

TEACHING

When it happened...
AD 30

Where it happened...
Jerusalem and the surrounding areas, Galilee

MAJOR THEMES

JESUS' RESURRECTION WAS AN END AND A BEGINNING. Jesus taught before his death, but his followers grasped only so much. The likely problem was that they expected him to physically assume David's throne and reign. So for forty days, the resurrected Christ left no doubt that he was alive and that his ministry on earth had only begun.

A POWERLESS CHURCH IS NOT THE CHURCH AT ALL. The disciples were not left to muddle along in their own strength as they spread the good news about Jesus. Jesus had promised that he would send the Holy Spirit to empower them to speak and to know what to say. This immersion (baptism) in the Holy Spirit would happen in Jerusalem.

WE ARE IN ADVERTISING, NOT MANAGEMENT. Some of the biggest questions of believers today are those dealing with Jesus' promised second coming. This was also a concern of the apostles. Jesus' answer to them is also an answer to us. It is God's job, not ours, to decide when that day occurs. Our job is to go into the world to prepare people for his coming.

ITS PART IN GOD'S PLAN

The promised Messiah had come. Jesus had died to pay humankind's debt. He was raised from death so that the same will happen for all who trust him. Before the apostles were ready to embark on the mission of building the kingdom of God, they needed to learn and to wait. The power unleashed by Jesus to energize the church was coming!

AD **30**
Jesus ascends into Heaven

AD **30** The disciples choose Matthias to join them in place of Judas Iscariot

Goliath challenged Saul's army for 40 days before David answered his challenge.

God, through the prophet Jonah, gave the city of Nineveh 40 days to repent.

Jesus spent 40 days in the wilderness before beginning his ministry.

Fifty days after Passover, Jews again gathered in Jerusalem for Pentecost. The apostles waited in Jerusalem as Jesus had commanded. The Spirit, with the appearance of fiery tongues, came upon them, and they began speaking in

THE CHURCH

When it happened...
AD 30

Where it happened...
Jerusalem

THE SPIRIT OF GOD MAKES ORDINARY PEOPLE POWERFUL. The idea that a handful of uneducated fishermen would change the world might have seemed ridiculous days earlier. But Jews who gathered in Jerusalem for one of the three pilgrimage festivals heard the message of Jesus in their native dialects, spoken by men who had never studied those languages!

THE LAST DAYS ARE NOW. The Day of Pentecost celebrated the commandments given to the Israelites through Moses—the old covenant. But on this day, the Holy Spirit who lived within those who followed Jesus would deliver the Word of God. This was the beginning of God's final covenant with humankind, the new covenant predicted by the prophets.

THE MESSAGE OF THE CHURCH IS COMPELLING. The miraculous coming of the Spirit was followed by a passionate and logical sermon delivered by Peter. When the church speaks with both indisputable power and reasonable polemic, the message is heard. Three thousand responded to Peter's call to follow Jesus and were baptized that day.

ITS PART IN GOD'S PLAN

Jews scattered all over the world would return to the temple to celebrate the festivals of Tabernacles, Passover, and Pentecost. Many people who had witnessed Jesus' crucifixion were again in Jerusalem. This time they learned the purpose of that sacrifice and were called to follow the resurrected Jesus.

AD **30** The Holy Spirit comes upon the church on the Day of Pentecost

JON NOVUNO

languages they had never learned. The international crowd listened as Peter explained what was happening, and three thousand were baptized for the forgiveness of sins and the gift of the Holy Spirit.

BEGINS

DAILY READING PLAN

October 7: Acts 2:1-13
October 8: Acts 2:14-36
October 9: Acts 2:37-41

AD **30** Peter preaches the first gospel sermon

AD **30** 3,000 people are baptized in response to Peter's sermon

This day is celebrated as a public holiday (Pentecost Monday) in these countries today:

Austria	Estonia	Luxembourg	Portugal
Belgium	France	Netherlands	Romania
Cyprus	Germany	Norway	Spain
Denmark	Hungary	Poland	Switzerland

*This new group of followers of Jesus worshiped together in the temple courts.
On one occasion, a man born with a disability was miraculously healed. The
man caused a great disturbance in his celebration, and a crowd gathered. Peter*

THE CHURCH

DAILY READING PLAN

October 10: Acts 2:42-47

October 11: Acts 3:1-10

October 12: Acts 3:11-26

October 13: Acts 4:1-22

October 14: Acts 4:23-31

October 15: Acts 5:17-42

From AD 30 The church
in Jerusalem continues to
meet in the temple courts

AD 30 Peter and John
heal a disabled man
at the temple gates

Sometime between
AD **28–75** Buddhism
introduced in China

explained how the man was healed, which brought joy to listeners but drew the ire of some members of the Sanhedrin. Peter and John were arrested while they were still speaking to onlookers.

AT WORSHIP

When it happened...
From AD 30

Where it happened...
Jerusalem

MAJOR THEMES

CHRISTIANITY IS COMPLETED JUDAISM. The first Christians were Jews. They worshiped with their countrymen. But their worship was no longer in anticipation of a coming Messiah. It had become the celebration of the kingdom of God among them.

THE CHURCH TOOK ADVANTAGE OF OPPORTUNITIES. God authenticated the words of the apostles with undeniable miracles. When a miracle occurred, such as the healing of a disabled man at the temple gates, it was explained with a sermon. The apostles would declare how the power that was displayed was not their own but was God fulfilling what he had promised to their ancestors.

THE CHURCH ACCEPTED PERSECUTION. The first persecution of the church came from the sect of the Sadducees. The undeniable miracles performed through the apostles threatened their authority. The apostles taught that the miracles came from the resurrected Jesus, and the Sadducees taught that one could not be resurrected from the dead. But the apostles, when threatened with more persecution if they were not silent, accepted the consequences. They could not keep silent.

ITS PART IN GOD'S PLAN

The apostles did not immediately build a new building and gather the new believers to worship there. That would assume that they were adherents to a new religion. Their message to their countrymen was not to stop being Jewish. Their message was that the Messiah had come and had begun to rule.

AD 30 The Sadducees have Peter and John arrested

From AD 30 The believers pray for boldness and continue to preach and teach

Sometime between AD 80–100 Jews at the Council of Jamnia may have discussed which books make up the Hebrew Scriptures

As the church grew in numbers, opposition grew as well. It was vital that the church be unified. Members met together, sharing meals and providing for one another's needs. They listened to apostolic teaching and shared the Lord's Supper together. When believers who were Greek-speaking Jews felt snubbed by

THE CHURCH

DAILY READING PLAN

October 16: Acts 4:32-37
October 17: Acts 5:1-11
October 18: Acts 5:12-16
October 19: Acts 6:1-7

When it happened...
AD 30–35

Where it happened...
Jerusalem

AD **30–35** The church
in Jerusalem faces
persecution

AD **30–35** The church in
Jerusalem becomes a tight-
knit community

Throughout history people have tried to build the ideal community:

The Amish—Followers of Swiss Mennonite leader Jakob Amman began creating self-governing religious communities in Pennsylvania in the 18th century. They exist throughout the U.S. today.

Kibbutzim—Self-governing Jewish agricultural communities began in the early 20th century in Israel. Both agricultural and urban kibbutzim continue to exist.

believers who were Hebrew-speaking Jews, the apostles examined the way goods were distributed and allowed for new leadership to emerge. When Ananias and Sapphira threatened the unity of the believers, God dealt with them decisively.

IN ACTION

MAJOR THEMES

THE HOLY SPIRIT UNIFIED THE CHURCH. Under the guidance of the Holy Spirit, the church was shaped into a community. By sharing their goods with one another, the early church began to erase socio-economic distinctions. By being dedicated to the teaching of the apostles, they became intellectually united. By sharing the Lord's Supper together, they recognized that they were one in spirit.

THE HOLY SPIRIT CORRECTED THE CHURCH. Nothing breaks the unity of God's people like false piety and deceit. Although the judgment of Ananias and Sapphira was sudden and severe, it was necessary. Lying to one another and trying to demonstrate moral superiority destroy the community God seeks to build. Before doing anything that will harm the church, we must stop and remember that God loved the church so much that his Son died for her.

THE HOLY SPIRIT EXPANDED THE CHURCH. Even the apostles were not above correction. When the apostles' fairness in food distribution was challenged, the Spirit would not allow them to act autocratically and suppress dissent. They asked the people to choose those servants who would distribute food, which would also allow the twelve apostles to be free to spread the gospel.

ITS PART IN GOD'S PLAN

The actual communal structure of the church in Jerusalem did not become the norm as the church expanded, but the principles that drove it did. The Holy Spirit would continue to mold, correct, and expand the church, as new barriers were soon to be broken.

Sometime between AD 30–35
Ananias and Sapphira are judged for lying to the Holy Spirit

AD 35 Seven leaders are chosen to help distribute goods within the church

Socialist communities—Welsh social reformer Robert Owen envisioned a utopian community in New Harmony, Indiana. The experiment was established in 1825 and dissolved in 1829 due to constant infighting.

Secular communities—Twin Oaks Community in Louisa County, Virginia, was founded in 1967 and has a population of around 100. They are supported by community businesses (such as making tofu) and hold to the core values of nonviolence, egalitarianism, feminism, and ecology.

The seven servers chosen by the Jerusalem church did more than distribute goods to believers. They also defended the gospel. This led to the execution of one server and the persecution of believers. But because they were forced out of Jerusalem, the gospel was spread throughout Judea and into Samaria. Peter was called to preach

PETER AND

When it happened...
Sometime between AD 35–45

Where it happened...
Caesarea

MAJOR THEMES

GOD DEFINES *VICTORY* DIFFERENTLY THAN WE DO. Stephen, one of the Jerusalem servers, had a name that literally meant "victor's crown." But Stephen's victory was his execution! As a result, however, Philip (one of the seven) began to preach in Samaria and even baptized a man returning to Africa. Others went as far as Phoenicia. Peter was amazed when God accepted Gentiles into his kingdom. A dark act was turned to triumph!

GOD CAN DO THE SAME THING MORE THAN ONCE. Peter was uneasy when the Holy Spirit directed him to a place he had been taught to consider ceremonially unclean—the home of a Gentile. But shortly after he arrived, the Holy Spirit came upon Cornelius's household and friends, causing them to speak in tongues just as the apostles had done on the Day of Pentecost. Peter then began to understand how wide the reach of God was!

GOD WORKS IN DIFFERENT PLACES AT THE SAME TIME. Apparently unrelated to Peter's visit to Cornelius, other believers went to Antioch and also invited Gentiles to follow Jesus. The apostles did not seem to authorize this beforehand. But the Holy Spirit moved these believers just as he moved Peter.

DAILY READING PLAN

October 20: Acts 8:4-25
October 21: Acts 8:26-40
October 22: Acts 10:1-23

October 23: Acts 10:24-48
October 24: Acts 11:1-18
October 25: Acts 11:19-21

**Sometime between
AD 32–35**
Stephen is executed

c. AD 32–35
Persecution breaks out,
scattering the church

c. AD 32–35
Philip preaches
in Samaria

c. AD 30 Water-powered
bellows and iron furnace
developed in China

DALL·ORTO

AD 37 Roman emperor
Tiberius dies, Caligula
succeeds

to a Gentile (non-Jew) soldier named Cornelius. At Cornelius's home the events of Pentecost were mirrored, opening the doors for the expansion of the church. Some believers scattered as far as Antioch in Phoenicia, welcoming Jews and Gentiles into the church.

CORNELIUS

ITS PART IN GOD'S PLAN

Before Jesus ascended into Heaven, he commanded the apostles to go to Jerusalem, Judea, Samaria, and the rest of the world. Some years had passed, but the church remained fairly isolated in Jerusalem! Persecution was not God's idea, but he used it to move the church beyond one spot and to empower believers to begin to fulfill their mission.

Sometime between AD **32–35**
Philip preaches to a man returning to Ethiopia

Sometime between AD **35–45**
Peter preaches at Cornelius's house

c. AD **35–45**
A church of Jews and Gentiles grows in Antioch

AD **41** Roman emperor Caligula murdered, Claudius succeeds

c. AD **41–54** Ambassador Rachias sent from Sri Lanka to the court of Claudius

Jewish opposition to the church seemed to grow. When Herod Agrippa, Roman ruler for the area, saw this, he had James the apostle beheaded. Getting a positive response from the Jews, Agrippa imprisoned Peter, holding him for execution after Passover. But on the day before Peter's execution, God answered the prayers of the

PETER IN PRISON

DAILY READING PLAN

October 26: Acts 12:1-11
October 27: Acts 12:12-19a
October 28: Acts 12:19b-24

Sometime between AD 35–44
Herod Agrippa I executes the apostle James, son of Zebedee

Sometime between AD 35–44
Herod Agrippa I arrests Peter

Too many Herods?
A number of Roman appointees named Herod ruled Palestine during the time of Jesus and the early church:

Herod the Great (74–4 BC)
renovated the temple and also was responsible for the slaughter of innocents after Jesus' birth.

Herod Archelaus (23 BC–AD 18),
son of Herod the Great, was ruler of Judea and Samaria when Mary, Joseph, and Jesus returned from Egypt. They moved to Galilee to avoid him.

church and sent an angel to free Peter. After both Peter and the church came to grips with this miracle, Peter left the area. Later, Agrippa's arrogance would be punished when an angel took his life.

When it happened...	Where it happened...
Sometime between AD 35–44	Jerusalem

MAJOR THEMES

IS AN ENEMY'S ENEMY A FRIEND? The Sadducees opposed the believers because they preached resurrection of the dead. The Pharisees also believed in resurrection, so they opposed the Sadducees. But when the church accepted Gentiles, the two sects had a common enemy, albeit for different reasons. The Roman leadership was regularly at odds with the Jews, but Herod won their favor by also attacking the church.

GOD EVEN SURPRISES BELIEVERS! The humor of Peter's prison escape is evident. Peter believed in the saving power of God, yet thought he was dreaming when an angel led him from prison. The church gathered to pray for Peter's release, but told the servant who said Peter was at the door that she must be mistaken. The power of God is beyond even a sanctified imagination!

EVEN THE BEST LEADERS MUST MOVE ON. Peter was indeed a pillar of the church in Jerusalem. But because he was now a wanted fugitive, he moved from the area. The next time the Bible speaks of the church in Jerusalem, it appears that James, the half brother of Jesus, had a major leadership role. Peter returned to Jerusalem later for a short time, but God had someone to take his place in Jerusalem and had other places where Peter was needed.

ITS PART IN GOD'S PLAN

The Sadducees appear to have been the Jewish sect most hostile to the church in the early years. But when the church began to include Gentiles, the Pharisees would certainly have been enraged too. Yet increased opposition, even when agents of the most powerful nation on earth joined in, could not overcome God's power. Peter escaped. His guards were executed. Herod was struck down. And the reach of the gospel increased!

Sometime between AD 35–44
An angel frees Peter from prison

AD 44
Herod Agrippa I dies

Herod Antipas (20 BC– c. AD 40) mocked Jesus and ordered the death of John the Baptist. He was also the son of Herod the Great.

Herod Agrippa I (c. 10 BC– AD 44), grandson of Herod the Great, had James executed and Peter imprisoned.

Herod Agrippa II (c. AD 27–100) was the son of Agrippa I and the last of the Herodians.

After Stephen was chosen as one of the seven servers in the Jerusalem church, members of the Synagogue of the Freedmen debated with him. They could not compete with the godly wisdom of Stephen, so synagogue members used false witnesses

PAUL AND THE

DAILY READING PLAN

October 29: Acts 6:8-15

October 30: Acts 7:1–8:2

October 31: Acts 22:1-3; 26:4-8

November 1: Philippians 3:1-6

When it happened...
Sometime between AD 32–35

Where it happened...
Jerusalem

c. 4th century BC Tarsus becomes known as a center of philosophy, poetry, and linguistics

66 BC Residents of Tarsus granted Roman citizenship

41 BC Cleopatra and Mark Antony first meet in Tarsus

to frame him. When asked to defend himself before the Sanhedrin, Stephen defended the gospel instead. He was stoned to death, and a young man named Saul of Tarsus (later called Paul) approved of his death.

EXECUTION OF STEPHEN

ITS PART IN GOD'S PLAN

Stephen's death was followed by increased persecution of the church and resulted in spreading the gospel beyond Jerusalem. It also inflamed the religious zeal of a young rabbi who would take a crucial role in the campaign against Jesus and the church.

MAJOR THEMES

THE HOLY SPIRIT MAKES US LIKE JESUS. One qualification for the seven servers was that each be full of the Holy Spirit. We see this in the miracles Stephen performed. But could the work of the Holy Spirit be responsible for the parallels between the life of Jesus and the life of Stephen? Both were framed by false witnesses. Both were accused with similar false charges. And both even spoke the same words at their executions!

WE NEED TO SAY WHAT MATTERS. When brought before the Sanhedrin, Stephen was asked whether the accusations were true. It may seem strange that Stephen did not answer that question! Instead, he used his opportunity to offer a reasoned articulation of the message of Jesus and the church. His argument that God lived in his people, not a building, would be repeated over and over as the church went into all the world.

RELIGIOUS ZEAL CAN BE DEADLY. Presumably, Saul of Tarsus was a member of this synagogue. Although Pharisees promoted a very strict moral code, these standards quickly disintegrated when long-held religious views were successfully challenged. Piety quickly gave way to bribery, agitated crowds, and the execution of an innocent man.

c. 5 BC Saul (Paul) born in Tarsus, capital of the province of Cilicia (in modern-day Turkey)

c. AD 25–35 Saul educated and rises to prominence as a Pharisee

Sometime between AD 32–35 Stephen executed

Following the death of Stephen, Saul of Tarsus began a deliberate campaign to destroy the church. He received authority from the Sanhedrin to enter synagogues and go door-to-door to arrest, imprison, and even execute those who would not deny that Jesus was the promised Messiah.

PAUL, THE

MAJOR THEMES

MISGUIDED ZEAL HAS NO LIMITS. When we look at religious zealots today, we are often repulsed when they target places of worship, private residences, and even innocent women and children. But Saul's zeal drove him also to enter synagogues, go door-to-door, and arrest men and women.

MISGUIDED ZEAL HAS NO BOUNDARIES. Religious zealots today certainly do not stay "in their own backyards"! The same was true with Saul. The Sanhedrin had been given very limited power over very limited real estate. But Saul had the nerve to ask the council to extend their reach far beyond Jerusalem. And they obviously agreed to do so.

MISGUIDED ZEAL HAS NO MERCY. Today we still speak of those who try to "convert by the sword." In other words, religious zealots may offer someone the choice between recanting—denying his beliefs—or dying. Saul would later confess that he tried to make people "blaspheme" and would raise his voice to agree to their executions if they did not do so.

ITS PART IN GOD'S PLAN

The power of God is shown when the most unlikely candidates turn to him. Saul of Tarsus was a headstrong, zealous, and even violent opponent of the church of Christ Jesus. His investment in opposing the church was so great that it seemed unlikely that anything on this earth could change his views. But someone *above* this earth could—and did!

c. AD 32–35
Saul (Paul) persecutes
the church

AD 64–68
Nero persecutes
Christians in Rome.

AD 177 Persecution of
Christians in Lyon
includes mob violence,
assault, and robbery.

DAILY READING PLAN

November 2: Acts 8:3; 9:1, 2

November 3: Acts 22:4, 5; 26:1-12

November 4: Galatians 1:13, 14; 1 Timothy 1:12-14

PERSECUTOR OF
THE CHURCH

When it happened...
c. AD 32–35

Where it happened...
Jerusalem and a very wide
surrounding area

AD **303–313** Emperor Diocletian legally rescinds rights of Christians in the Roman Empire, leading to widespread persecution and execution of Christians.

AD **1789** The so-called Dechristianisation of France by leaders of the French Revolution leads to the deportation and even execution of clergy.

While Saul was traveling to Damascus to persecute the church, Jesus appeared and spoke to him. Saul was struck blind and was ordered to meet Ananias, a believer from Damascus. After Ananias restored Saul's sight, Saul was baptized, ate some food, and regained his strength.

PAUL BECOMES

DAILY READING PLAN

November 5: Acts 9:1-9; 22:6-11
November 6: Acts 9:10-19a; 22:12-16
November 7: Galatians 1:15-24
November 8: Acts 9:19b-31; 22:17-21
November 9: Acts 11:19-30

c. AD 35 Saul of Tarsus (Paul) meets Jesus on the way to Damascus

c. AD 35 Saul meets Ananias at the house of Judas

c. AD 35 Saul goes to Arabia

c. AD 38 Saul returns to Damascus

History tells of other unlikely converts to Christianity:

Augustine of Hippo (AD 354–430), a pagan intellectual, converted to Christianity and became an effective theologian.

Lew Wallace (AD 1827–1905), an influential statesman, was asked to write a book disproving Christianity once and for all. In the process he became a Christian and penned the novel *Ben-Hur*.

Saul fled to Arabia, later returned to Damascus, and finally met with church leaders in Jerusalem. He went home to Tarsus, where he remained until Barnabas sent for him to help minister in the Antioch church, which contained both Jewish and Gentile believers.

A CHRISTIAN

MAJOR THEMES

ATTACKING THE CHURCH IS ATTACKING JESUS. On the road to Damascus, Jesus asked why Saul was persecuting him. Jesus takes attacks on the church personally! We do well to remember that harsh treatment of Christians from inside or outside the church is an attack on those whom Jesus literally loves to death.

GOD ASKS BELIEVERS TO TAKE BIG RISKS. Christians knew of the relentless campaign of Saul against the church. When God told Ananias of Damascus to go to the place Saul was staying, he was justifiably concerned. Why would God ask a Christian to befriend such a dangerous man? But Ananias took the risk, and history would be changed.

CHRISTIANS ARE CALLED TO GOD'S TIMETABLE, NOT THEIR OWN. God would use Saul in remarkable ways. But after Saul's first attempts to teach others about Jesus, he was run out of town! To protect him, the church in Jerusalem sent Saul back to his hometown, where he remained until Barnabas sent for him a few years later. But the wait was worth it.

ITS PART IN GOD'S PLAN

Saul of Tarsus would become one of the most prominent figures in the church of the first century. But it took time before Saul the persecutor became Paul the apostle and teacher in the church in Antioch. And that was only the beginning.

When it happened...
c. AD 35

Where it happened...
On a road outside Damascus (present-day Syria) and later, Straight Street in Damascus

c. AD 38 Saul visits church leaders in Jerusalem

c. AD 38 Saul returns to Tarsus

c. AD 45 Barnabas seeks Saul to work with him in Antioch

C. S. Lewis (AD 1898–1963) was an outspoken atheist intellectual who embraced Christianity. His books, including *Mere Christianity* and The Chronicles of Narnia series, continue to influence generations of believers.

Charles Colson (AD 1931–) was a ruthless politician under President Nixon and was imprisoned for his part in the Watergate scandal. Since coming to Christ, he has written many powerful books and founded Prison Fellowship, a worldwide ministry.

The Holy Spirit directed the leaders of the Antioch church to send Paul and Barnabas on a mission trip. They began by preaching in synagogues in Cyprus, Galatia, and Phrygia. On a second trip, Paul took Silas to the churches established on the first trip but desired to go farther. After trying to enter new territory but being

PAUL BECOMES

When it happened...
AD 47–58

Where it happened...
Across the Mediterranean region

ITS PART IN GOD'S PLAN

Paul planted churches throughout the Mediterranean world. Since most of these were in larger cities, visitors who heard him in those places went back home and started offshoots of those churches in their smaller towns. In little more than a decade, the gospel spread throughout the Roman Empire.

AD 47–49 Paul's first missionary journey

AD 52–54 Paul's second missionary journey

Famous modern-day missionaries:

William Carey (1761–1834), the Father of Modern Missions, worked in India for 41 years and translated the Bible into numerous languages.

David Livingstone (1813–1873) was a pioneer medical missionary, as well as an explorer, in Africa.

unsuccessful, Paul had a vision of a man from Macedonia (northern Greece). Paul and Silas established churches in Macedonia and Achaia (southern Greece) before returning home. On a third journey Paul revisited some of those churches and spent an extended time in Ephesus, the second largest city of the Roman Empire.

A MISSIONARY

MAJOR THEMES

KEEP YOUR BAGS PACKED. The work at the church of Antioch was going well—so well that Paul and Barnabas were no longer needed there! The leaders sent them off to repeat their successes in areas in which the gospel had not yet been preached.

KEEP YOUR PLANS FLEXIBLE. Paul consistently went to large cities in which there was a synagogue. But when Paul set his sights on cities in Bithynia and Asia, things just did not work out. Instead of stubbornly forcing his will, Paul waited for guidance. He received that guidance in a vision directing him to Macedonia.

KEEP DOING WHAT WORKS. The leaders at Antioch sent Paul on his first missionary journey. But the other two trips seem to have come from his past successes and his desire to follow up on those and expand his reach. Sometimes we receive clear direction from God through leaders or circumstances. But lacking that, it is wise to follow our passions and experience.

DAILY READING PLAN

November 10: Acts 13

November 11: Acts 14

November 12: Acts 15:36–16:10

November 13: Acts 16:11-40

November 14: Acts 17

November 15: Acts 18:1-23

November 16: Acts 19

November 17: Acts 20

c. AD 52 Paul has a vision calling him to Macedonia

AD 54–58 Paul's third missionary journey

James Hudson Taylor (1832–1905), known for his total faith in God's provision, was a missionary to China for 51 years and founded the China Inland Mission.

Gladys Aylward (1902–1970) evangelized while assisting the Chinese government in enforcing the law against foot-binding young girls.

Elisabeth Elliot (1926–) was a missionary to the Waodani people in Ecuador after they killed her missionary husband and four others.

The missionary work of Paul and Barnabas sparked a controversy in the early church. Gentiles, who for the most part had not been taught to follow the Law of Moses, were considered to have a lower standard of morality than Jews. Some

A CONTROVERSY

When it happened...
AD 51

Where it happened...
Jerusalem

ITS PART IN GOD'S PLAN

The first false teaching to arise in the church was an attempt to hold on to Judaism. By getting together and allowing the Holy Spirit to work within them corporately, those on opposing sides of the controversy were brought to unity. This allowed them to clarify their message as it continued to spread into Gentile territory.

Sometime between AD 49–51
Some believers from Jerusalem go to Gentile churches to challenge Paul

Sometime between AD 49–51
Paul writes the letter to the Galatians to answer the controversy

In the centuries after Paul's day, church leaders would continue to meet to address controversies:

Council of Nicaea (AD 325) responded to Arius, who taught that Jesus was not God but created by God. The church clarified that Jesus is "of one substance with the Father."

argued that in order to keep the church as morally pure as possible, Gentiles would need to become Jews (by being circumcised according to the Law) before becoming Christians. A council was called in Jerusalem to settle the matter.

IS ADDRESSED

MAJOR THEMES

RESIST A DESIRE TO CONTROL. The common wisdom teaches that the purpose of religion is to control members of society with the threat of an ever-present and all-seeing God. But God's reason for sending Peter to Cornelius was not to tell Cornelius how to live. Rather, God sent Peter to show *Peter* that the Holy Spirit was available to all. Real control does not come from outward rules but through inward rebirth.

LOOK IN THE MIRROR. Human beings enforcing rules from the outside can, at best, only create a society that has the same strengths and weaknesses as the human leaders. Peter recognized that even the best of Jesus' followers were unable to perfectly keep the Law. Why should they expect others to do better than they had?

COMMUNICATE CLEARLY. The Gentile churches were confused, and rightly so. Paul and Barnabas taught that they were saved by grace. Some others came from Jerusalem and taught that law keeping was a prerequisite before grace could be granted. Therefore, the decision makers put the verdict in writing and sent two men (who possibly were at one time on opposite sides of the issue!) to deliver it face-to-face.

DAILY READING PLAN

November 18: Galatians 1:6-10

November 19: Galatians 2

November 20: Galatians 3:1-25

November 21: Galatians 3:26–4:7

November 22: Galatians 5

November 23: Galatians 6

November 24: Acts 15:1-35

AD 51 A church council meets in Jerusalem to clarify the message that needed to be preached in Gentile churches

First Council of Constantinople (AD 381) continued to respond to Arius and affirmed that the Holy Spirit was also of the same substance as the Father.

Council of Ephesus (AD 431) and Council of Chalcedon (AD 451) discussed how Jesus' humanity and divinity interacted within him during his earthly life.

As Paul traveled and planted new churches, he also kept in touch with churches he had started, as well as those he hoped to visit in the future. Paul had been driven out of Thessalonica after a very short time, so he wrote to give further instruction.

PAUL'S LETTERS

When it happened...
AD 52–58

Where it happened...
At various stops on Paul's missionary journeys

AD **52** Paul writes
1 Thessalonians from
Corinth

AD **52** Paul writes
2 Thessalonians from
Corinth

If the messages of Paul's
early letters were summarized
for fortune cookies, here's
what they might say:

Galatians—Legalists will try to steal the joy of your freedom.
1 Thessalonians—If you die before Jesus returns, you still get to go with him!
2 Thessalonians—May Jesus find you working hard for him when he returns.

Paul heard disturbing reports from the church he had started in Corinth, so he gave strong counsel as needed. Paul had not founded the church in Rome, the capital of the empire, but he longed to visit and expressed those desires in a letter.

MAJOR THEMES

THOSE NEW TO THE FAITH NEED ENCOURAGEMENT AND CORRECTION. Paul seemed almost shocked that the Thessalonian church, whose early days were marked with unrest and arrests, survived at all! But there was confusion about how and when the world would end and how believers should behave in the meantime. Two letters of encouragement helped clarify that.

THOSE IN AN IMMORAL SOCIETY NEED UNITY. Even in a morally challenged Greek culture, the city of Corinth was considered to be lacking in restraint and civility. The Corinthians embraced the message of salvation by grace and almost took it to the point of license. The church of Corinth was marked with selfishness and headstrong independence that nearly splintered it to bits. Some even attempted to discredit Paul and take on his role.

THOSE WE HAVE YET TO MEET NEED TO KNOW WHAT WE BELIEVE. One could almost envision Paul looking west and imagining a trip to Rome and western Europe. The letter to the Romans is actually a complex theological treatise spelling out Paul's view of salvation, as well as advice about how Jewish and Gentile Christians could work together. He also expressed his wish for them to help finance a planned mission trip to Spain.

DAILY READING PLAN

November 25: 1 Thessalonians 2:17–3:6
November 26: 1 Thessalonians 4:13-18
November 27: 2 Thessalonians 3:6-14

November 28: 1 Corinthians 1:10-17; 3:1-11; 10:23, 24, 31-33
November 29: 2 Corinthians 13
November 30: Romans 1:11-17; 3:21-31; 6:1-14

ITS PART IN GOD'S PLAN

The Holy Spirit working within the church soon caused believers to recognize that the letters of Paul and the other apostles were more than just friendly notes. They were prophetic words with relevance for the church in every place and for all time. Individual congregations began making copies of these letters for other congregations and collecting these writings to be studied along with Old Testament Scripture.

AD 55 Paul writes 1 Corinthians from Ephesus

AD 57 Paul writes 2 Corinthians from Macedonia

AD 58 Paul writes Romans, anticipating visiting there for the first time

1 Corinthians—It's not about you! Take care of one another!
2 Corinthians—See 1 Corinthians.
Romans—Salvation comes to Jews and Gentiles the same way: God does it!

When Paul returned to Jerusalem after his third missionary journey, he was accused of defiling the temple. A riot broke out, and he was arrested and taken to Caesarea. As a Roman citizen, he took advantage of his right to ask for a trial before Caesar and was sent to Rome, where he was placed under house arrest. There he continued to write

PAUL'S

When it happened...
AD 61–68

Where it happened...
Rome

AD **58** Paul arrested in Jerusalem

AD **61** Paul sent to Rome to be tried before Caesar

AD **61–63** Paul under house arrest in Rome

AD **63** Paul writes letters to the Ephesians, Philippians, Colossians, and Philemon

c. AD **50** Emperor Claudius orders Jews to leave Rome

to churches he had directly or indirectly started. Apparently, Paul was released and continued to minister to churches. He gave leadership advice to two of his protégés, Timothy and Titus. It is believed that Paul was rearrested as persecution of Christians in Rome grew more heated. He wrote a final letter to Timothy as he awaited execution.

IMPRISONMENT IN ROME

EVERY SITUATION IS AN OPPORTUNITY. While imprisoned, Paul was in the constant company of Roman guards. In Paul's mind, it was the guards who were the captives, not him! The palace guards soon came to know what Paul believed and were convinced that he was innocent of treason. In addition, other believers, seeing that it was possible to thrive while being imprisoned, were themselves emboldened to spread the good news about Jesus.

GOOD LEADERS PASS THE TORCH. No leader will live on this earth forever. Paul wisely recruited and trained others to continue the work he had begun. He further counseled that they also look for others that they could train, allowing the gospel to penetrate even more deeply into the world.

ENDING WELL IS IMPORTANT. Toward the end of his second imprisonment, Paul knew his days were numbered. Yet he would continue to work until the end. He asked that friends be sent to assist him and to bring warmer clothing and study materials. He looked back on his life as a race well run—and looked toward his execution without regrets.

ITS PART IN GOD'S PLAN

The once zealous rabbi became a servant. The once rabid persecutor of the church became a martyr. Yet those chapters of Paul's life between his conversion and execution were lived to the full, strengthening the church and equipping believers to follow his example.

AD 65–66
Paul writes letters of
advice to ministers
Timothy and Titus

AD 67–68
Paul's second
imprisonment

AD 67 Paul writes
2 Timothy in
anticipation of his death

AD 68
Paul executed
by Nero

AD 64 Great Fire of
Rome used as a reason
for Emperor Nero to
persecute Christians

AD 68 Nero
commits suicide

During the early years of the church, the apostles recounted eyewitness testimony of Jesus' life and authenticated their message with undeniable miracles. Soon a basic outline of the life of Jesus began to be learned and passed

LIFE OF JESUS

ITS PART IN GOD'S PLAN

Because Matthew, Mark, and Luke cover roughly the same events, they are often referred to as the *Synoptic* Gospels, meaning "having the same view." Each author included additional touches, however, based on his own experiences, research, and original audience.

When it happened...
Sometime between AD 50–70

Where it happened...
Various locations

Sometime between AD 50–70
Matthew writes his Gospel

Artists would later use specific symbols for these three writers:

Matthew is symbolized as an angel proclaiming that Jesus would be Immanuel, God with us.

on among believers. But as the gospel spread throughout the world, it became advisable to have these testimonies in written form. The first three Gospels were written during this time.

RECORDED

MAJOR THEMES

JESUS IS THE MESSIAH PROMISED TO THE JEWS. Jewish Christians did not see Jesus as one who began a new religion, but one who fulfilled the promises of the prophets. Matthew appealed to them by beginning with a genealogy that showed Jesus to be a descendant of Abraham and one sought by wise men as a promised king. These readers would have seen similarities between Jesus and Moses, such as an escape as an infant from a genocidal ruler and bringing mountaintop messages from God.

JESUS WAS SENT BY GOD TO ACT DECISIVELY AND WITH POWER. Mark knew the disciples well and is thought to have gotten much information from Peter. Mark appealed to the Roman mind with his short, action-packed account. Many think he shared a laugh at his own expense by including the account of a young man (Mark himself?) who fled naked after Jesus was arrested!

JESUS WAS THE COMPASSIONATE RESCUER OF A WORLD THAT COULD NOT SAVE ITSELF. Luke may hold the distinction of being the only biblical writer who was not Jewish. It's possible he obtained information from Mary the mother of Jesus, as well as from many other eyewitnesses. He was a physician who traveled with Paul on parts of his missionary journeys (and also wrote the book of Acts). Luke's Gospel includes the stories of Jesus' care for those marginalized by society—shepherds, women, Samaritans, and the poor.

DAILY READING PLAN

Sometime between AD 50–65
Mark writes his Gospel

Sometime between AD 59–63
Luke writes his Gospel and the book of Acts

Mark begins his Gospel with John the Baptist "roaring" in the desert, so Mark is often symbolized as a courageous lion.

Luke is represented as a sacrificial animal—a bull. The account of Zechariah the priest begins Luke's Gospel.

The first major controversy in the church came from Jewish believers and was addressed at the Jerusalem council. But as the church pushed westward, controversies arose from those trained in Greek philosophies and religions. Paul addressed an early

FALSE TEACHING

When it happened...
AD 63–67

Where it happened...
Various locations

ITS PART IN GOD'S PLAN

The church will always be tempted to follow the ideas and behaviors of those around us, even to the extent of trying to incorporate false ideas into our teaching. But the counsel of the early disciples and the continuing work of the Holy Spirit can help bring correction.

AD **63** Paul confronts a peculiar blend of Jewish and Greek false teaching with his letter to the Colossians

Sometime between AD **64–68** 2 Peter written to condemn false teaching

c. AD **65** Jude, another half brother of Jesus, discusses similar false teaching

AD **50** Philo, a Jewish philosopher who tried to harmonize Judaism with Greek thought, dies

"reinvention" of Jesus in the town of Colosse. Later in Ephesus he helped Timothy battle false teaching that tried to incorporate Greek thought into the message of Jesus. Peter and Jude also responded strongly to teachings that would undermine the true gospel.

IS CONFRONTED

AD 65 or 66 Paul writes 1 Timothy and addresses certain false teaching in Ephesus

AD 67 Paul writes 2 Timothy and addresses another false teaching in Ephesus

c. AD 77–79 Pliny the Elder publishes an early encyclopedia, *Naturalis Historia*

AD 93–94 Josephus writes *Antiquities of the Jews*

James, the half brother of Jesus and a leader in the Jerusalem church, wrote to encourage Jewish Christians scattered around the known world. The book of Hebrews (attributed by many to Paul although it is unsigned) also addressed Jewish

THE CHURCH

When it happened...
Sometime between AD 40–70

Where it happened...
Various locations

DAILY READING PLAN
December 23: James 1:2-8; 2:5-7; 5:7-20
December 24: Hebrews 1:1-4; 3:1-6; 4:14-16; 11:32–12:11
December 25: 1 Peter 3:8-22; 4:7-19

Sometime between AD 40–50
James encourages Jewish Christians with practical advice for living out their faith

27 BC The Roman senate awards the emperor the title of Caesar *Augustus* ("the revered one"), giving the emperor the right to be worshiped as a god.

AD 40 Roman emperor Caligula orders that an idol of his likeness be placed in the temple at Jerusalem, but is later persuaded to change his mind.

Christians, arguing that Jesus was superior to Moses, angels, and the priesthood. Peter wrote to Christians who were fearful of coming persecution, urging them to continue serving God faithfully.

IS ENCOURAGED

ITS PART IN GOD'S PLAN

The full power of Rome was not turned on the entire church until the latter part of the first century, but life was not easy for the first believers. Jewish Christians faced hatred from the Greco-Roman world in addition to social and economic isolation from the Jewish community. Rumors of Nero's persecution of Christians in Rome caused believers to anticipate a widespread purge. But Spirit-led followers of Christ encouraged the church with letters that were soon passed from congregation to congregation.

Sometime between AD 60–64 1 Peter is written to encourage Christians (in many congregations started by Paul) not to fear persecution

AD 66–73 First Jewish-Roman War results in the destruction of the temple and death of Jewish insurgents.

Sometime between AD 60–70 The book of Hebrews encourages Jewish Christians not to return to Judaism

AD 79 Mount Vesuvius erupts, destroying the Roman cities of Pompeii and Herculaneum.

John, the son of Zebedee, outlived his fellow apostles. In his later years he resided in Ephesus, the second largest city of the Roman Empire at the time. When some teachers challenged the church by mixing Greek philosophy with Christian thought, John wrote another account of Jesus' life and three letters to answer that challenge.

THE LAST LIVING

ITS PART IN GOD'S PLAN

About six decades after Jesus' resurrection, the apostle John was still telling about it! His teaching inspired faith in Jesus and assurance of the salvation Jesus brings, because it came from an eyewitness. To this day the church battles against those who would reinvent Jesus to be more of what they want him to be. But the words of these first-century eyewitnesses continue to correct the myths and keep the teachings of the church reliable.

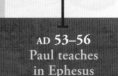

AD **53–56**
Paul teaches
in Ephesus

AD **68**
Peter and Paul
executed
by Nero

Sometime between
AD **35–44** Herod
Agrippa I executes
the apostle James,
son of Zebedee

APOSTLE WRITES

When it happened...
Sometime between AD 80–95

Where it happened...
Ephesus

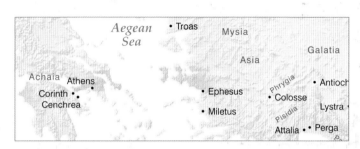

Aegean Sea • Troas   Mysia
Achaia Athens   Galatia
Corinth •   Asia
Cenchrea   • Ephesus   Phrygia   • Antioch
    • Colosse
    • Miletus   Pisidia   Lystra
        Attalia • • Perga

MAJOR THEMES

JESUS IS NOT A MYTH. John opened his first letter by affirming that Jesus was a flesh-and-blood person. Jesus was divine, but he was not a ghost or an illusion. While John's opponents were speculating that Jesus might have been some kind of otherworldly being, John countered, saying that he and the other disciples knew Jesus as someone their eyes saw, their ears heard, and their hands touched. God did indeed take human form.

SIN IS INEVITABLE YET UNDESIRABLE. The false teachers in John's day claimed to know Jesus because of some sort of special revelation. This special knowledge, in their estimation, set them apart from others and even from the moral standards of God! John countered that no one is free from sin. But he continued to argue that arrangements had been made to forgive sin.

BECAUSE WE ARE LOVED, WE CAN LOVE OTHERS. The false teachers argued that the distinguishing mark of a true believer was special knowledge from God. But a claim of special or greater knowledge only causes division. John recalled and repeated the words of Jesus on the matter. The distinguishing mark of the church would be the sacrificial love believers have for one another.

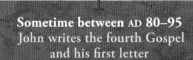

Sometime between AD 80–95
John writes the fourth Gospel and his first letter

Sometime between AD 85–95
John writes his second and third letters

c. AD 69–155 Life of Polycarp of Smyrna, a church leader taught by John

c. 99 Death of Clement of Rome, a church leader taught by Peter

In addition to threats from within the church, there was a growing threat from without. Roman emperor Domitian enforced a policy of emperor worship during AD 81–96. Since Christians refused to worship a man, widespread

JOHN HAS A VISION

DAILY READING PLAN

December 29: Revelation 1:9–3:22

December 31: Revelation 21, 22

December 30: Revelation 12, 13

JESUS REMAINS PRESENT WITH HIS CHURCH. The book of Revelation is filled with vivid word pictures. Individual churches are described as lamps, sending the light of Jesus' message to the world. Jesus is pictured as one who walks among those lamps, tending the flames. Even in the darkest times, the church has light, and Jesus is present to keep it lit!

SATAN USES HUMAN LEADERS TO HARASS THE CHURCH. The ancient serpent who deceived Adam and Eve in the beginning will be around until the end. John pictures Satan as a great dragon bent on destroying the church. In John's vision, the dragon empowers an ugly beast wearing royal crowns to persecute the church. But the fate of this beast is certain. Human leaders may harass the church, but they will be destroyed.

THE INHERITANCE OF ADAM AND EVE WILL BE OURS AGAIN. When Adam and Eve rebelled against God, they were evicted from their perfect home. But because Jesus paid the price of that rebellion, the descendants of Adam and Eve will again have access to paradise. The tree of life, once in the middle of Eden, will have a prominent place in the New Jerusalem John described.

ITS PART IN GOD'S PLAN

Christians differ in their beliefs as to the details of Jesus' return to earth. But the fact remains that he *will* return! In the meantime we are comforted by the promise of Jesus' presence, empowered by his inevitable victory, and excited at the prospect that we will live forever in his presence!

Throughout the ages, there have been mistaken ideas about the end of time:

First Millennium Christians—In AD 999, it is said, Europeans expected Jesus to return as the year 1000 began. Some partied, some gave their belongings away, and others traveled to meet Jesus in Jerusalem.

The Millerites—In 1843–44, more than 50,000 followers of William Miller abandoned their material possessions, went to the hills of the northeastern United States . . . and waited for the world to end.

persecution of the church began. John was exiled to a small island where Jesus gave him a special vision of the future, rich with images from Israel's past, that continues to encourage the church to this day.

OF THE END

When it happened...
c. AD 95

Where it happened...
The island of Patmos off the coast of Ephesus

Sometime between
AD 90–95 John in exile
on the island of Patmos

c. AD 95 John
writes Revelation

Heaven's Gate—As the Hale-Bopp comet approached the earth in 1997, the Heaven's Gate cult taught that aliens hidden in the comet would take members away with them. In preparation, 39 cult members prepared for that event by carrying out a mass suicide.

Hutaree—In 2010, the FBI arrested members of a survivalist group for plotting to kill police officers. The Hutaree were readying to war with the U.S. government as preparation for Jesus' return.

JESUS, THE IMAGE OF GOD

How can Jesus *be* God, yet be *separate* from God? This seems confusing. We talk about Jesus being God, but he prayed to God. Jesus died, but God does not die! How can this be if there is only one God?

The Bible talks about Jesus being the image of God who contains everything that is God (Colossians 1:15-20). *Image* is an important word in the Bible. Image is more than just a drawing or a reflection. It is the model for the drawing and the essence of that which is reflected.

First, your image does not go away when a receptor is not present. Think of it this way: You look at yourself in a mirror. Someone behind you throws a rock and shatters the mirror. Your image was not destroyed, only the receptor of it. Imagine that behind the first mirror are a million more mirrors. When the first mirror is destroyed, your image remains and is reflected on the next mirror.

Next, your image does not change because of the nature of the receptor. Look at yourself in a mud puddle, a shiny piece of metal, and then a full-length mirror. You look different in each. But your *image* is the same in the biblical sense of that word. The receptors of that image are what vary in quality.

Take it one step further. Imagine a "supermirror." It not only has perfect clarity but also reflects your image 360 degrees and all the way through you. It captures and reflects every molecule of your being. Should that be the case, that image would be the equivalent of you. But it was *not* created—it flowed from you. Your image is equal to you, but it is not a separate being. It would not exist were it not from you.

God is perfect. Therefore, he is a perfect reflector. His self-image (Jesus) is flawless and is equal to and flows from himself. That image is not a separate God. He is everything God is.

IS THE NEW TESTAMENT GOD DIFFERENT FROM THE OLD TESTAMENT GOD?

You've probably heard that question before. In fact, it has been asked for almost nineteen centuries! The gist of the question is whether or not the nature or personality of God is different in the Old Testament than in the New Testament.

To clarify this question, let's ask another. Is your father a different person today than he was when you were a child? Of course, he has physically aged, but his general personality is probably about the same as it was decades ago. Nevertheless, his interactions with you are much different now than they were back then. But *he* did not change. *You* did!

When we were children, our fathers disciplined us. They made restrictive rules for us to follow. They limited our freedom. But in our adulthood, our parents may still have the role of adviser, but they no longer discipline, make restrictive rules, or otherwise limit our freedom. The change in approach is based on a difference in our maturity.

This is not a perfect comparison to God, but it is illustrative. We must remember the great gap between humankind and God after Adam and Eve. People were changed to such an extent that God had to reintroduce himself slowly and systematically.

The Old Testament books were written over centuries. Noah had none of them! Neither did Abraham! Moses wrote the first books, but the subsequent books had not been written. David knew more than Moses. The later kings were told still more. By the time of the prophet Malachi, the knowledge of God and what he expects was so much clearer than it had been centuries before.

If we were to imagine our fathers treating us the same way today as they did when we were five years old, we would certainly think them to be tyrants! But the demonstrative, directive, and disciplinary actions of our fathers in those days were necessary for us in our state of maturity. In a similar (although not totally the same) way, the God of the Old Testament did act in some different ways than he does now. But he has not changed.

IF GOD IS LOVE,
WHY IS THERE A HELL?

The Bible talks about the existence of Hell, using such terms as the *second death,* the *lake of fire,* and the *outer darkness* (Revelation 21:8; 20:14; Matthew 25:30). Nevertheless, the Bible doesn't talk about how it came to be, nor does it give a great deal of detail on the subject. Therefore, much that is popularly believed about Hell comes from speculation or outright fantasy.

The idea that Hell is the domain of Satan has more in common with classic literature and popular myth than the Bible. The Bible does *not* speak of Hell as a kingdom in which the devil rules and tortures the souls of humans who go there. In fact, the Bible talks about Hell as *punishment* for Satan and his angels (Matthew 25:41; Revelation 20:10)!

Perhaps it is helpful to look at an example with which we are more familiar. Consider darkness. Darkness cannot be created; light can only be extinguished. Consistently in Scripture God is referred to as light. Hell is referred to as the outer darkness, having absolutely no light. So we might describe Hell as the result of God's withdrawing his presence completely.

Therefore, the question of people going to Hell is a question of whether or not part of the image of God within humans is eternal. In this age, God is here—like it or not! We have no choice. It is up to us to acknowledge him and desire to know him more completely. Or not. But as this age ends, and assuming that man's spirit is eternal, that eternal spirit would continue to exist (Daniel 12:2; 1 John 5:13; Revelation 6:9). But without the presence of God and the goodness that comes from him, how horrible that existence would be!

Looking at it this way, we see that God does *not* send people to Hell. In fact, we know he does all he can to coax people to spend eternity in his presence (John 3:16, 17; 1 Timothy 2:3, 4; 2 Peter 3:9). But he does not force us to accept his offer. In the same way that we choose darkness by not turning on a light, we send *ourselves* to Hell by not choosing to spend eternity with God.

WHY IS THE CHURCH CALLED THE *BRIDE OF CHRIST*?

At first glance, this phrase seems a little strange—perhaps even a little gender-bending, since women and *men* are in the church! But it is a crucial concept. It is also linked with another title of Jesus—Redeemer (Galatians 3:13, for example).

Society in ancient days was very dependent on men working the land. A woman without family members to work the land could be in deep trouble! Imagine a case in which a couple working their land has yet to have children. With presumably his best years still ahead, the man is murdered. The widow has no one to work the land, soon goes into debt, loses her land, and is reduced to poverty. She also lives in fear that the enemy who took her husband's life will come back for her.

In the Law of Israel, God provided for what was called a kinsman-redeemer (Ruth 2:20). This redeemer was the late husband's closest available male relative of means. He had three tasks to perform:

1. He was the redeemer. He redeemed (bought back) the widow's property by paying her debts.

2. He was the avenger. He made sure that the murderer of her late husband was brought to justice, never to harass her again.

3. He was the groom. He married the widow, bringing her back into the family.

This strange societal practice was really an illustration of the human dilemma. Humankind lost their inheritance due to the malevolence of Satan in the Garden of Eden. Immediately after their rebellion, Adam and Eve were evicted. The Bible even talks about the entrance back into the garden being barred by force (Genesis 3:24)! They also were in danger of future attacks by the enemy. Finally, they lost the family name. The special privileges of being children of God no longer belonged to Adam and Eve.

The role of kinsman-redeemer also was an illustration of what Jesus would do. Jesus would pay the price to buy back paradise. When he gave his life, the debts that made the Garden of Eden off limits were paid. He would then totally defeat Satan. No longer would those who belonged to Jesus have to fear that Satan could take them against their will. Then Jesus would give the church his name along with all the rights of being back in the family of God!

The New Testament also uses the illustration of human marriage to be a picture of Christ and his bride, the church. Read more about this in Ephesians 5:1, 2, 22-33; Revelation 19 (especially vv. 7-9), Revelation 21 (especially v. 9), and Revelation 22 (especially v. 17).

SON OF GOD OR SON OF MAN?

If Jesus is the Son of God, why did he often call himself the Son of Man? In recent days this has become an argument used by those who would deny the divinity of Christ. It is in effect saying that later writers called Jesus divine (Son of God) but that he saw himself as an ordinary human being.

The phrase *son of man* is a meaningful Hebrew expression. It is true that it commonly meant "ordinary guy" or, as an old English expression goes, "every mother's son."

We see that usage often in the Old Testament. For example, Psalm 8:4: "What is man, that thou art mindful of him? and the son of man, that thou visitest him?" This is a typical Hebrew parallelism (a repetition to emphasize a point). Another example is found in Numbers 23:19: "God is not a man, that he should lie; neither the son of man, that he should repent." These words of Balaam simply meant that God is not like a typical human being.

In Ezekiel, God referred to Ezekiel as "son of man." In other words, he was saying that the great prophet was just an ordinary person to whom God had given an important message (Ezekiel 2:1, 3, 6, 8, etc.).

But the term *Son of Man* became an important Messianic title. God told the prophet Daniel that someone who appeared to be an "ordinary Joe" would be sent by God and be given absolute authority and eternal rule over all nations:

"I saw in the night visions, and, behold, one like the Son of man came with the clouds of heaven, and came to the Ancient of days, and they brought him near before him. And there was given him dominion, and glory, and a kingdom, that all people, nations, and languages, should serve him: his dominion is an everlasting dominion, which shall not pass away, and his kingdom that which shall not be destroyed" (Daniel 7:13, 14).

Therefore, the term *Son of Man* was seen as a very important Messianic title. It was one Jesus used for himself over and over again in the New Testament (for example, Luke 5:24; Matthew 25:31). Jesus was not just saying that he had a human parent. He was claiming to be this divine and eternal king with authority equal to God's. Some would argue that *Son of Man* was an even stronger claim to divinity than was *Son of God*!

AREN'T ALL RELIGIONS BASICALLY THE SAME?

The world's most influential religions are: Hinduism, Judaism, Buddhism, Christianity, and Islam. While having some similarities, there are distinct differences.

CHRISTIANITY AND RELIGIONS OF THE FAR EAST (HINDUISM AND BUDDHISM)

What is God like?—Christianity and Eastern religions hold very different views of God. It may surprise many, but much of Buddhism does not recognize a god at all! Other sects of Buddhism and some sects of Hinduism are polytheistic (recognizing a variety of gods and goddesses). Eastern religions also may be pantheistic (believing that God is an impersonal force found in everything in nature) and/or monistic (believing that all that exists is God). Christianity, in contrast, worships a single, personal God. Christians do not see God as an impersonal force but as having attributes of a person, such as consciousness, intelligence, and creativity.

Does the world make sense?—Eastern religions usually see the world as unreal, irrational, or possibly evil. Therefore, they often see a necessity for transcending, escaping, and even denying the reality of the natural world. Christianity sees the world as a creation of an intelligent, good, and logical God. The world, though not everything God intended it to be (because of human rebellion), is still beautiful, knowable, and can be enjoyed. Christianity, more than teaching the need to find an escape from the world, seeks to find a person's place in the world and in God's plans.

CHRISTIANITY AND RELIGIONS OF THE MIDDLE EAST (JUDAISM AND ISLAM)

What does God want?—Judaism, Christianity, and Islam disagree with Eastern religions about the nature of God and this world. There is also much agreement between these three religions on morality, the standards of right and wrong for humankind. Yet a major difference lies in their views of humanity. Judaism and Islam see human beings as capable of living either morally or immorally. For that reason, they find it possible to win God's favor by following his moral commands. Christianity, while acknowledging that people can choose to do right or wrong, believes that human nature is so fundamentally flawed that we can never fully follow God's commands or pay the penalty for those commands we break. Christianity teaches that Jesus pays for our wrongdoing and grants us a new nature that allows us to follow God more perfectly.

Who are God's people?—Judaism traces its beginning to Abraham through his son Isaac. Islam traces its beginning to Abraham through his son Ishmael. While there are Jews and Muslims all over the world, both religions retain a strong ethnic element. Christianity has no such element. Jesus calls people to follow him regardless of nationality, race, or ethnicity.

See the bibliography for books that compare Christianity with other religions.

HUMOR IN THE BIBLE

The Bible can give us a good chuckle now and then. Here are some examples of the types of humor found in Scripture.

PUNS

A common device in humor is to play on words that have different meanings but sound similar. We have all heard that a newspaper is "black and white and *read* all over." Someone might joke, "I'm so bright, my mother calls me *son*." (OK, they are not *great* jokes!) We sometimes miss the puns included in the Bible because they are lost in translation. But they are in there! Here are a few:

Jeremiah 1:11, 12—God promised Jeremiah that he was watching by showing him a branch of an almond tree. (Huh?) The word for almond tree *(shaqed)* sounds like the word for watching *(shoqed)*.

Amos 8:2—To warn the prophet Amos that Israel was about to be conquered, God showed him a basket of summer (overripe) fruit and told him that the end was near. The word for summer fruit *(qayits)* sounds like the word for end *(qets)*.

Philippians 4:2, 18—Paul thanked the Philippians for the gifts they sent him, calling them a sweet-smelling, or fragrant, offering. Some think this was a clever way to thank a woman in the church who was responsible in some way for the gifts. The woman's name, Euodia, literally meant "fragrant."

Philemon 10, 11—Paul converted the escaped slave of Philemon to Christ. Paul joked that the slave, Onesimus (whose name meant "useful"), had been useless to Philemon but had become very useful (another Greek word) because of his conversion.

IRONY

American short story writer O. Henry is known for his use of this device. Henry's stories would end with an unexpected twist. Some surprise endings that O. Henry would have been proud to claim are found in the Bible.

Absalom—This son of David rose to popularity, at least to an extent, because of his fabulous head of hair (2 Samuel 14:25, 26). Absalom successfully exploited his charm and good looks to get others to join him in a rebellion against his father (15:12). Ironically, Absalom's mane became his downfall when his head got caught in a tree as he, while riding a mule, was fleeing from David's soldiers (18:9, 15)!

Haman—As a power-hungry officer of Xerxes of Persia, Haman was infuriated by the fact that a Jew named Mordecai would not bow to him. Haman had a seventy-five-foot gallows built and planned to have Mordecai executed on it (Esther 5:9-14). Unaware that his enemy was the foster father of the queen, Haman met his end by being hanged on the very gallows he had intended for Mordecai (7:1-10)!

HUMOROUS IMAGERY

Sometimes we use figures of speech to paint a ridiculous word picture. We may say that a jumpy person acts like he has "ants in his pants" or that a person suffering an allergy attack might "sneeze his head off." Similar uses of humorous imagery can be found throughout the Bible.

Hosea—The prophet was describing the nation of Israel that got itself in trouble by not fully following God's commands. Hosea said that the nation was like flatbread that was cooked only on one side (Hosea 7:8). We still use the term *half-baked* to describe behavior that has not been thought through.

Solomon—The writings of King Solomon are filled with this type of zinger. Solomon described a beautiful woman with a less-than-beautiful character as being like a golden ring that was placed in a pig's snout (Proverbs 11:22).

Warning against the danger of trying to referee a domestic dispute, Solomon compared it to trying to hold a dog by the ears (26:17), an apt description of a no-win situation. Once you irritate a dog in that way, you can't hold on long, but it is also dangerous to let go!

Jesus—In one of his most famous sayings, Jesus talked about the foolishness of trying to offer advice without dealing with one's own faults. He pictured someone trying to remove sawdust from another person's eye when he had a log in his own eye (Matthew 7:3-5)!

SARCASM

It is said that ridicule is the lowest form of argument. But some folks are so foolish that they deserve to be laughed out of town!

Elijah—When the prophet Elijah sought to prove that Israel was following false gods, he devised a contest (1 Kings 18:16-39). He, as a prophet of the true God, would set up an altar with a sacrifice on it, and the prophets of the false god Baal would do likewise. Both would ask their respective deity to send fire to burn up the sacrifice. When watching the prophets of Baal frantically dance and shout to no avail, Elijah taunted them into yelling louder. He sarcastically suggested that Baal was taking a nap or out of town!

Jesus—When faced with the ridiculous behavior of the Jewish leaders, even Jesus responded by poking fun at their expense. On one occasion, Jesus healed a man who had been born blind (John 9). The miracle was obvious. But instead of believing, some wanted to say that the sighted man only looked like the blind man. When the evidence mounted, the Pharisees tried to win their argument with a display of raw power—excommunicating any who disagreed with them. Jesus stood next to the healed man and sarcastically joked that the foolish leaders were blinder than the man *ever* was!

OUTRAGEOUS SITUATIONS

Situations that go from bad to worse can be fraught with humor. This is especially true when they are happening to someone else! Slapstick humor featuring one pratfall after another is this type of comedy. When God intervened in human affairs, he could not help but become a part of some outrageously funny situations.

Elisha and the Arameans (Syrians)—A prophet can be a great military ally! One such account is recorded in 2 Kings 6:8-23. When the king of Syria plotted to ambush the king of Israel, God would tell Elisha where the enemy was lying in wait. Elisha would warn the king of Israel, foiling the plot time after time. Finally, the king of Syria caught on to what was happening and sent an army to capture the prophet.

While the army was on the way, God struck the entire group with blindness. Elisha came up to those who were sent to find him and offered to give them directions. Unaware of what was happening, the Syrians were led right into the clutches of the army of Israel by the man they were sent to capture! Adding insult to injury, the king of Israel held a party in the honor of the captured army, wined and dined them, and sent them back home. One could only imagine the reaction of the king of Syria upon hearing that embarrassing tale!

Peter and Rhoda—One could hardly imagine a funnier story than the account in Acts 12:1-16. Peter was in prison, awaiting execution. The church met at the house of Mary, praying for a miraculous release. When God answered that prayer by sending an angel to set Peter free, even Peter had a hard time believing it. Although he was a wanted fugitive, Peter decided that he needed to tell the church of his miraculous escape. When he arrived at Mary's house, a servant girl named Rhoda went to answer the door. Recognizing Peter's voice through the door, she was so shocked that she immediately ran to tell the others—leaving him outside and exposed to those he feared were pursuing him!

Inside, the story became even more ridiculous. Instead of running to the man for whose rescue they prayed, the pious, praying church began to argue among themselves. The servant, they surmised, was mistaken or imagining things. The servant continued to testify to what she knew. All the while, Peter remained outside, knocking frantically!

Surprised by all the humorous stories in the Bible? There are plenty more where those came from! Dig around in the Scriptures, and you'll discover a guy who fell asleep during a sermon and toppled out of the third-floor window, phony exorcists who couldn't fool the demon, a newly chosen king hiding among the baggage . . .

20 EVERYDAY EXPRESSIONS THAT COME FROM THE BIBLE

The Bible is such an influential book, it has actually changed the way we talk! Here are some common English expressions that have their roots in the Bible. These references all come from the *King James Version* of the Bible, translated in 1611.

1. **Apple of my eye**
   Definition: The named person is very dear to me.
   Psalm 17:8—Keep me as the apple of the eye, hide me under the shadow of thy wings.

2. **At wit's end**
   Definition: The named person is emotionally unable to cope with a situation.
   Psalm 107:27—They reel to and fro, and stagger like a drunken man, and are at their wit's end.

3. **Be sure your sin will find you out**
   Definition: It is better to be caught before bad behavior escalates.
   Numbers 32:23—Behold, ye have sinned against the LORD: and be sure your sin will find you out.

4. **Can't tell left from right**
   Definition: The named person is confused or is out of touch with reality.
   Jonah 4:11—Should not I spare Nineveh, that great city, wherein are more than sixscore thousand persons that cannot discern between their right hand and their left hand . . . ?

5. **Don't know if I'm coming or going**
   Definition: I am so overwhelmed that I lack direction in the task before me.
   1 Kings 3:7—And now, O LORD my God, thou hast made thy servant king instead of David my father: and I am but a little child: I know not how to go out or come in.

6. **Drop in the bucket**
   Definition: The named item is so small as to be inconsequential.
   Isaiah 40:15—Behold, the nations are as a drop of a bucket, and are counted as the small dust of the balance: behold, he taketh up the isles as a very little thing.

7. **Fly in the ointment**
   Definition: The named item, while small, ruins everything.
   Ecclesiastes 10:1—Dead flies cause the ointment of the apothecary to send forth a stinking savor: so doth a little folly him that is in reputation for wisdom and honor.

8. **Gave up the ghost**
   Definition: The named person died, or the named item has ceased to function.

Acts 12:23—And immediately the angel of the Lord smote him, because he gave not God the glory: and he was eaten of worms, and gave up the ghost.

9. **A house divided**
Definition: Internal conflicts within a group will destroy it.
This phrase is probably best known as coming from a famous speech delivered by Abraham Lincoln in Springfield, Illinois, on June 16, 1858: "A house divided against itself cannot stand. I believe this government cannot endure permanently half slave and half free."
Matthew 12:25—Jesus knew their thoughts, and said unto them, Every kingdom divided against itself is brought to desolation; and every city or house divided against itself shall not stand.

10. **How the mighty have fallen**
Definition: The once powerful have suffered defeat.
2 Samuel 1:27—How are the mighty fallen, and the weapons of war perished!

11. **Let justice roll down like water**
Definition: May right behavior totally wash away evil.
This phrase is probably best known as coming from the famous "I Have a Dream" speech delivered by Dr. Martin Luther King Jr. on the steps of the Lincoln Memorial in Washington, D.C., on August 28, 1963: "No, no, we are not satisfied, and we will not be satisfied until justice rolls down like waters and righteousness like a mighty stream."
Amos 5:24—But let judgment run down as waters, and righteousness as a mighty stream.

12. **A little bird told me**
Definition: I obtained information from an unnamed source.
Ecclesiastes 10:20—Curse not the king, no not in thy thought; and curse not the rich in thy bedchamber: for a bird of the air shall carry the voice, and that which hath wings shall tell the matter.

13. **A man after my own heart**
Definition: The named person shares my views.
1 Samuel 13:14—But now thy kingdom shall not continue: the LORD hath sought him a man after his own heart, and the LORD hath commanded him to be captain over his people, because thou hast not kept that which the LORD commanded thee.

14. **My brother's keeper**
Definition: I am responsible for the well-being of another.
Genesis 4:9—And the LORD said unto Cain, Where is Abel thy brother? And he said, I know not: Am I my brother's keeper?

15. **No rest for the wicked**

    Definition: People who do evil will suffer.

    Isaiah 57:20, 21—But the wicked are like the troubled sea, when it cannot rest, whose waters cast up mire and dirt. There is no peace, saith my God, to the wicked.

16. **Nothing new under the sun**

    Definition: Every idea has been considered before.

    Ecclesiastes 1:9—The thing that hath been, it is that which shall be; and that which is done is that which shall be done: and there is no new thing under the sun.

17. **Old as the hills**

    Definition: The said person or item has extreme age.

    Job 15:7—Art thou the first man that was born? Or wast thou made before the hills?

18. **Scapegoat**

    Definition: The said person takes the blame for an entire group.

    Leviticus 16:9, 10—Aaron shall bring the goat upon which the LORD's lot fell, and offer him for a sin offering. But the goat, on which the lot fell to be the scapegoat, shall be presented alive before the LORD, to make an atonement with him, and to let him go for a scapegoat into the wilderness.

19. **Scattered to the four winds**

    Definition: The said items or people are all over the place.

    Jeremiah 49:36—Upon Elam will I bring the four winds from the four quarters of heaven, and will scatter them toward all those winds; and there shall be no nation whither the outcasts of Elam shall not come.

20. **Skin of my teeth**

    Definition: I have barely been able to accomplish said task.

    Job 19:20—My bone cleaveth to my skin and to my flesh, and I am escaped with the skin of my teeth.

BIBLIOGRAPHY

BOOKS

Ankerberg, John, Don Weldon, and Dillon Burroughs. *The Facts on World Religions.* The Facts On Series. Eugene, OR: Harvest House Publishers, 2004.

Bickel, Bruce, and Stan Jantz. *World Religions and Cults 101: A Guide to Spiritual Beliefs.* Eugene, OR: Harvest House Publishers, 2002.

Carden, Paul, ed. *Christianity, Cults & Religions.* Rose Bible Basics. Torrance, CA: Rose Publishing, 2008.

Christianity Today International. *Crash Course on the New Testament.* Cincinnati: Standard Publishing, 2008.

Christianity Today International. *Crash Course on the Old Testament.* Cincinnati: Standard Publishing, 2008.

Grun, Bernard. *The Timetables of History.* 4th ed. New York: Simon & Schuster, 2004.

Life Application Bible: New International Version. Wheaton, IL: Tyndale House Publishers, 1991.

McDowell, Josh, and Don Stewart. *Handbook of Today's Religions.* Nashville: Thomas Nelson, 1996.

New Testament Maps and Charts. Cincinnati: Standard Publishing, 2000.

Old Testament Maps and Charts. Cincinnati: Standard Publishing, 2000.

Root, Orrin. *Training for Service: Leader's Guide.* Rev. ed. Cincinnati: Standard Publishing, 1996.

Standard Bible Atlas. Cincinnati: Standard Publishing, 2008.

WEB SITES

Absolute Astronomy. "Solar Eclipse Timeline." http://www.absoluteastronomy.com/timeline/Solar_eclipse.

All Experts. "Mythical Origins of Language." http://en.allexperts.com/e/m/my/mythical_origins_of_language.htm.

Amazing Bible History Timeline. "Amazing Bible Timeline with World History e-Chart." http://Bibletimeline.net.

Ancient Mediterranean. "The Ancient Mediterranean from 10,000 BC to 700 AD." http://tam.ancient.eu.com/timeline.

Apologetics Press. "Internet Sacred Text Archive." http://www.apologeticspress.org.

British Museum: Explore World Cultures. "Ancient Egypt." http://www.britishmuseum.org/explore/world_cultures/africa/ancient_egypt.aspx.

Carnegie Museum of Natural History. "Life in Ancient Egypt: Chronology of Ancient Egypt." http://www.carnegiemnh.org/exhibitions/egypt/chronology.htm.

Chronological Bible Time Line. "Bible Time Line: Part 2 (2343 BC–1446 BC)." http://www.abiblestudy.com/part2.html.

Early Jewish Writings. "Philo of Alexandria." http://www.earlyjewishwritings.com/philo.html.

E-History Archive. "Timeline—Ancient History: 12,000 BC to 500 AD." http://ehistory.osu.edu/world/TimeLineDisplay.cfm?Era_id=4.

Encyclopedia Britannica. http://www.britannica.com.

Eras of Elegance. "The Ancient Era: 4000 BC to 476 AD." http://www.erasofelegance.com/history/ancienttimeline.html.

EyeWitness to History. "The Assassination of Julius Caesar, 44 BC." http://www.eyewitnesstohistory.com/caesar2.htm.

Fordham University. "Medieval Sourcebook: The Persecution and Martyrdoms of Lyons in 177 AD." http://www.fordham.edu/halsall/source/177-lyonsmartyrs.html.

Freeman Institute. "Return to Glory: Ancient Egyptian Photo Gallery." http://www.freemaninstitute.com/RTGpix.htm.

Gates, Henry Louis Jr. "Black Kingdoms of the Nile." Wonders of the African World. http://www.pbs.org/wonders/fr_e1.htm.

Gill, N. S. "Alexander the Great Study Guide." About.com: Ancient/Classical History. http://ancienthistory.about.com/od/alexander/a/Alexander.htm.

Heli, Richard M. "Timeline of Carthaginian History." Phoenician Encyclopedia. http://phoenicia.org/carthtimeline.html.

History Today. "Explore History from the Earliest Times to the 21st Century." http://www.historytoday.com/TimeLine.aspx?m=3813&amid=3813&Start=-1500&End=-1000.

Hooker, Richard. "Egyptian Timeline." Washington State University, 1997. http://www.wsu.edu:8080/~dee/EGYPT/TIMELINE.HTM.

Indiana University. "Timeline for China to 1700." http://www.indiana.edu/~e232/Time1.html.

Institute of Egyptian Art and Archaeology: Selection of Ancient Egyptian Artifacts. University of Memphis. http://www.memphis.edu/egypt/artifact.php.

Internet Sacred Text Archive. "Nicene Creed." http://www.sacred-texts.com/chr/nicene.htm.

Jewish Virtual Library. "Ahab." http://www.jewishvirtuallibrary.org/jsource/biography/Ahab.html.

Konig, George, and Ray Konig. About Jesus, Christianity, and the Bible. "Bible History Timeline." http://www.konig.org/timeline.htm.

Oriental Institute of the University of Chicago. "Faces of Ancient Egypt." David and Alfred Smart Museum of Art, University of Chicago, 1996–1997. http://oi.uchicago.edu/gallery/faces.

Piccione, Peter A., PhD, Egyptologist, University of Charleston, History Courses. http://www.cofc.edu/~piccione/index.html.

Religion Facts. "History of the Amish." http://www.religionfacts.com/christianity/denominations/amish.htm.

Ruhlen, Merritt. "Where Do Languages Come From?" Exploratorium Magazine. Volume 23, Number 1. http://www.exploratorium.edu/exploring/language/index.html.

Tour Egypt. "Egypt Mythology." http://www.touregypt.net/gods1.htm.

Washington State University. "World Civilizations: An Internet Classroom and Anthology." http://www.wsu.edu:8080/~dee.

Web Chronology Project. "The Fall and Rise of Empires (1100–465 BC)." http://www.thenagain.info/webchron/Mediterranean/RiseEmpires.html.

Wholesome Words: Christian Biography Resources. "William Carey." http://www.wholesomewords.org/biography/biorpcarey.html.

Wikipedia: The Free Encyclopedia. http://en.wikipedia.org.